Mélange a Trois

Mélange a Trois

A poetry-prose anthology

**Larry L Ladd
Sharon S Gibson
Jim B Miller**

authorHOUSE®

AuthorHouse™ LLC
1663 Liberty Drive
Bloomington, IN 47403
www.authorhouse.com
Phone: 1-800-839-8640

© 2014 Larry L Ladd, Sharon S Gibson, Jim B Miller. All rights reserved.

No part of this book may be reproduced, stored in a retrieval system, or transmitted by any means without the written permission of the author.

Published by AuthorHouse 08/29/2014

ISBN: 978-1-4969-3569-4 (sc)

Any people depicted in stock imagery provided by Thinkstock are models, and such images are being used for illustrative purposes only.
Certain stock imagery © Thinkstock.

This book is printed on acid-free paper.

Because of the dynamic nature of the Internet, any web addresses or links contained in this book may have changed since publication and may no longer be valid. The views expressed in this work are solely those of the author and do not necessarily reflect the views of the publisher, and the publisher hereby disclaims any responsibility for them.

Dedication

To my son, Ryan Patrick Ladd,
whose love, generosity and encouragement
made this project possible.

ACKNOWLEDGEMENTS

I wish to thank my co-authors, Sharon Sue Gibson, of Kansas City, MO and James B. Miller, of Corpus Christi, TX. They contributed their considerable talent and limited time unselfishly helping me fill this book. I also want to thank my wife, Karen Jean O'Neal Ladd, for helping me organize the material for publication, and doing the lioness' share of the typing.

TABLE OF CONTENTS

CHAPTER ONE

Buddy & Rooster 3
The Day the Drugstore Died .9
The Orphan Pig 10
Lizard. 12
Style 13
Alphanumeric Anatomies 14
About Fear 15
Leftovers 16
Our Time 17
Little Poems One 18
Description (Fred K) 19
Milk & Cornbread 20
Mel Famey 21

CHAPTER TWO

I Am the Queen 25
Carole's Boxes 26
Float Trip 27
Fear Pays a Visit. 29
Little Poems Two 31
The Chase 32
Parkinson Song 33
History 35
Sometimes 36
Morning Rituals 37

Peggy Lee..38
Trial of the One-Eyed King........................40
Urban Battle...42
Rhinoceros..43
Billy Blue.. 44
Roy Rogers...45

CHAPTER THREE

Rafting...49
Black Holes..52
Winter..53
Mama's Jingle..54
Poets in the Room....................................55
The Lonely Hour......................................56
Verklempt...57
Ocean View..58
Afternoon Trains......................................59
Fortune's Favorite....................................60
Dance with the Dragon............................61
Little Poems Three...................................62
Wallpaper Redux......................................63
Strawberry... 64

CHAPTER FOUR

Asher..67
Sub-Urbia...72
Sharon's Theory.......................................74
Beauty..75
Verses from Vesuvius...............................76
Song of the Sailor....................................77

Pique-Nique 79
The Crabapple Tree 80
Lost Horizons. 81
Little Poems Four 82
Touché Cliché. 83
Secret Dissenters 84
Bird Bordello 85
Pavement 87

CHAPTER FIVE

Asher II 91
Mr. Frost's Cat 97
Thought or Prayer 98
Silent Lilacs 99
Winter's Midnight Trees 100
Peach 101
Lesson in Humility. 102
Bedpan Fans. 103
Ad Infinitum 104
Standing Orders. 105
Have Done So Much 106
Little Poems Five 107
Trompe L'oeil 108
Scapegoat. 109

CHAPTER SIX

Asher III. 113
Daisies Are Fine Company .119
Taps Plus One. 120
Flying Potatoes. 121

Song to Myself.............................123
The Autopsy...............................124
Little Poems Six...........................126
To a Texas Pothole........................127
Barren Tree...............................128
Cranes....................................129
Celibate..................................130
Love Is Relative...........................131
Divine Circumspection....................132
HODAR Salute............................133
Schmaltz..................................134
Benny....................................135

CHAPTER SEVEN

Uncle Coot...............................139
Parapraxis................................141
Little Poems Seven........................142
Let the Party.............................143
Exercise in Youth.........................144
Widows Walk............................145
Silhouette................................146
Father's History..........................148
Pledge Sunday...........................149
Trickledown Survivor.....................151
The Cat-astrophes........................152
Close Call................................153
The Burdens of Youth....................154
Disco....................................155

CHAPTER EIGHT

Cherchez La Femme 159
Japanese Tea Garden 163
I Think 164
Genius 165
The Lost Soles 166
Our Crisis 167
Fallen Trees 168
Psycho Chefs & Paranoid Potatoes 169
I Grow Old 170
Neighbor's Chimes 171
November 172
The Devil You Say 174
In Tune 175
Little Poems Eight 176
Sister Deloris 177
US Mail 179

CHAPTER NINE

Seashells 183
A Modest Fantasy 185
Chance Encounter 186
The Man Who Measured Time 187
Gravy in a Jar 188
The World Spins Its Bottle 190
Orinoco 192
Pieces 194
Little Poems Nine 195
The Fallen 196
Period 197

Facing Rejection................................198
Prayer Takes Many Forms......................200
Pliny's Curse 201
Teeth..202

CHAPTER TEN

When I Go 205
Ben Weir 206
mornings 208
Weevils..209
You Are What You Eat........................209
Angry Beachgoer...............................210
Choir 210
The Burial 211
Spring's Tree V 212
Little Poems Ten...............................213
Taps 214
While Waiting for the Bus & More 215
First Day Jitters 216
Seems Like Overkill To Me...................217
A Diabolical Diagram 218
Perks..219
Humility..220
This Is My Poem 221

CHAPTER ELEVEN

About the Authors 223
    Jim B. Miller................................223
    Sharon S. Gibson..........................224
    Larry L. Ladd 225

PREFACE

THERE WAS A MAN WITH A TONGUE OF WOOD

There was a man with a tongue of wood
Who essayed to sing,
And in truth it was lamentable,
But there was one who heard
The clip-clapper of this tongue of wood
And knew what the man
Wished to sing,
And with that the singer was content.

Stephen Crane

I gravitate toward the shorter poems. The shortest poem I know in English is entitled "Fleas".

Fleas

Adam
Had 'em

Author Unknown

The shortest poem I have created, I call "Camping Honeymoon".

Camping Honeymoon

Intense
Intimacy
In tents

I like this, because the words nest so easily together. Most of the poems I like are semi or actually funny. Some are just plain silly. Here is one I learned from Uncle John:

> My love has flew
> She done me dirt
> I did not knew
> She were a flirt
> To those unschooled
> I do forbid
> To be so done
> As I was did
> She has come
> She has gone
> She has left I all alone
> It cannot was
>
> Author unknown

My father-in-law had a couple of his favorites which he recited often.

> They do not let me drive the train
> Nor can I ring the bell
> But let the darned thing jump the tracks
> And guess who catches hell!
>
> I eat my peas with honey.
> I've done so all my life.
> It makes the peas taste funny,
> But it keeps them on my knife
>
> Authors unknown

Some short poems may be serious as well.

Alvin York became one of the most decorated American soldiers during WWI. He hailed from a Tennessee farming family. Audie Murphy grew up on a farm in Texas. He became one of the most decorated American soldiers during WWII.

TRIBUTE

Alvin York
Audie Murphy
Country boys

...LLL

The thing that has carried us this far is that we are having fun reading, writing and reciting verse. Ms SS Gibson and I were on the patio one afternoon when she proposed that we try to write a poem together. I was willing. She suggested that we alternate thinking up lines without discussing where the poem was going. So we began...
about halfway through we tried to determine whether our poem had rhyme or rhythm. Then we plunged ahead to its conclusion. This is what we created:

Ladies First

"Ladies first" he said,
as he stood aside.
"No don't defer to me", she cried.
He was aware of the form of her
but had not looked at her 'til now.
He looked, and tried not to scowl—
Was she a glass ceiling breaker,
pushing to get ahead?

If he couldn't get her in an elevator,
How could he get her in bed?
She saw the look in his eyes and sighed.
Is every door held by someone on the prowl?
Or was it all just in her head?
Anger grew at what his gesture implied.
But he stood quietly and tried to smile.
Was simple courtesy out of style?

Reluctantly, she stepped inside the door.
He followed and said, "What floor?"
She punched the button herself instead,
Which he took to mean, "Drop dead."
This was a woman headed to the top.
He heard the glass shards begin to drop.
He saw more now than a feminine form—
A self-reliant woman not deluded by his charm.

                                              ...LLL & SSG

We thought it remarkable that we actually created a poem in this manner.

We (Ladd-Gibson-Miller) have assembled this anthology in much the same way. We pooled our poems and other writings, culled through them and chose what we liked. We even allowed some short prose pieces to come aboard. We believe our efforts have created a patchwork quilt of poetic styles and content that you will enjoy and find thought provoking as well. May you find yourself listening for the clip-clapper of a tongue of wood that has opened your mind, touched your heart or stirred your soul.

Larry Ladd, aka LLL

Chapter One

Buddy & Rooster	LLL
The Day the Drugstore Died	SSG
The Orphan Pig	JBM
Lizard	SSG
Style	JBM
Alphanumeric Anatomies	LLL
About Fear	SSG
Leftovers	JBM
Our Time	SSG
Little Poems One	LLL
Description (Fred K)	SSG
Milk & Cornbread	JBM
Mel Famey	LLL

BUDDY & ROOSTER

They called me "Buddy" when I was small. I was named after my father, but no one called me "Junior". My mother did call me "Larry Junior" in a soft voice when she was talking with her friends and in a more strident, scolding tone when questioning me about some infraction, but no one called me "Junior".

I think Granny Whitfield started calling me "Buddy" and it stuck. My aunts, uncles and cousins on my mother's side still call me "Buddy", even though my father died over a decade ago and there is little chance of confusion. Somehow, I suspect, it's more than habit. Behind that nickname lies the idea that I am still that boy called "Buddy" forty years ago. It's as if my seldom-seen relatives are picking up a thread labeled "Buddy" to tie a few more memory knots on—never realizing that this "Buddy" is unquestionably different from the last time they saw him.

People are like that. They want to fix things, events and people in time by labeling them to hold them unchanged.

Take my friend, Andy. He's half my age now, but I've known him since he was 4. When he was younger, he called me "Ladd" because it was easier to say than "Larry". I can still hear him calling me "Ladd" as we drove across town. Andy would sit buckled in place in the back seat where I could watch him in the rearview mirror. I would begin to sing. I'm certain this is far more common than most men are willing to admit.

I've seen other grown men cruising along behind rolled up windows drumming on their steering wheels obviously performing their best Elvis or Johnny Mathis impersonations. My mistake was to sing out loud with Andy in the car, for he was sure to say, "Don't sing, Ladd. Don't sing." We never agreed on my singing, but we agreed on other things.

Andy was a St. Louis Cardinal fan; so was I. He liked hot dogs—in fact for a time, I think hot dogs were the only food he would eat. I liked hot dogs. Andy loved his dog, Gidget, and after a couple of years of her snarling and lunging at my calves as if they were Grade-A, number one prime New York strip steaks, we made our peace. I learned to like Gidget, but like enjoying the torrents of water plunging over Niagara Falls, liking Gidget was best done at a distance. Mostly Andy and I liked each other because he lived in the house behind ours and we saw each other a lot. So I watched Andy grow up, but in my mind he was a child even after he was grown. I seemed to forget or deny that Andy was becoming a man.

You see. Andy is a person others call "special", but not in the sense of a warm fuzzy specialness. He was born with a little bit of genetic material most of us lack. A third chromosome of the twenty-first kind where there should be only two and Down's syndrome results. Andy is what is termed mentally retarded, impaired, handicapped, deficient—all of which is to say that he learns at a much slower rate than most people. Also, his language skills developed more slowly, and this affected his social interactions. Physically, his reflexes were slower and baseball and running skills took a long time to achieve.

In fact, when Andy was born, Dr. Kinder told his father that he would never play ball and that he ought to be placed in a "special care facility" by which he meant an institution. But Andy's dad, who seldom spared an expletive, told Dr. Kinder what he could do with his prediction and suggestion and then went out to buy a baseball.

Some of my earliest memories of Andy are "baseball" highlights of his dad playing catch, showing him how to run and teaching him to bat with background music in the form of play-by-play commentary from a Cardinals game on the radio.

Andy had a shock of red hair that often stood on end when he took his ball cap off. This rumpled red comb earned him the nickname "Rooster." His dad would encourage him with, "Way to go, Rooster.", "Good swing, Rooster.", "Hustle out there, Rooster." And for a time, I was part of the inner circle of those allowed to call him "Rooster", but after his dad died of cancer I could not bring myself to use that nickname.

Andy never said anything, but in the weeks after the funeral, "Rooster" took on a new significance to me—a private nickname reserved to be used by a father with pride.

His father was proud of him and would have been even more so had he lived to see Andy grow to manhood. I imagine Andy's dad would have invited Dr. Kinder to be his guest at the Illinois State Special Olympics the first time Andy's team went to state. He definitely would have sent Dr. Kinder a Special Olympics Christmas card the year Andy's drawing of an ice skater was chosen as the cover design. But I'm fairly certain his motive and message would not truly have fit the season. Andy's dad would have thrown a tremendous back yard barbecue with strings of Chinese lanterns dancing in the Chestnut trees the night Andy graduated from high school. These were moments to be proud of the Rooster.

It's not that I wasn't proud of Andy at these times; I was. It's just that I wasn't allowing him to grow up in my mind. I thought of the times his fear of heights would get the better of him and he would sit down on the steps of the bleachers. Hundreds of people milling around and a football game in progress while Andy slowly backed up the steps one at a time so he would not have to look through the cracks to the ground beneath.

When you think about it, it's a reasonable concern. If more people looked through the cracks at what's under the bleachers, the stands would look like a bucket of crayfish backing into their seats.

To me Andy was still the kid who called from time to time to talk to "my good friend, Larry". He always told me the Cardinal scores in his slow, staccato way, "Cardinals win. The St. Louis Cardinals '7', the Philadelphia Phillies '5'. The Cardinals are in second place." I might need to ask a couple of times to understand his speech, but Andy was patient with me. Then he would ask to speak to his "good friend, Ryan" and soon I could hear the slap of a basketball on a backboard as the two boys shot baskets in Andy's back yard.

Andy continued to play ball with the Special Olympics and he was the catcher for the Methodist's men's slow pitch softball team. He often invited me and my wife, Karen, to watch his games. We would cheer for him and the Methodists—even when they played the Presbyterians. I mostly knew Andy from back yards, baseball games and bowling. I seldom thought of him as working, but he did.

Andy worked in his mother's flower shop. I'm told that he had more patience than most putting the little ribbon through the hole in the corner of each greeting card and tying it into place. He also unfolded and set up the corsage boxes and kept the workroom swept out. I would see him in the back room when I went into the shop, but I seldom thought of him as working.

I was still thinking of him going to the shop after school and waiting for his mom to take him home. I let myself forget that, at 24, Andy was no longer a schoolboy. But I was soon to be shaken out of my delusion.

One Saturday afternoon in July, we invited Andy to lunch. We were planning a vacation and Karen had hired Andy to bring in the mail and newspaper each day and water the plants when they needed it. I was on our deck grilling hot dogs when Andy stepped through the bushes into our back yard. "Hello, Larry," he said. "Hi, Andy. How you doing?" I replied. "Fine," he said as he climbed the stairs to the deck.

In a few minutes we were seated around a table holding grilled hot dogs, corn on the cob, potato chips and watermelon. When asked if he wanted anything else brought to the table, Andy pronounced, "Karen, you sit down. Larry it is…enough." We joined hands when I said, "Let's pray," and as is my habit I fell silent for a few seconds to compose myself. Before I could say anything I heard Andy begin to pray,...

"Our Father in Heaven..."

I thought, "Okay, we'll say the Lord's Prayer," but Andy went on in his own direction...

"Our Father in Heaven, this is my very best friend Karen. She is a good wife to Larry. She is a good mother to Ryan. Ryan is my very good friend. He is a graduate...he graduated high school. I like my best friend Ryan. This is my best friend Larry. He is a good father for Ryan and a good husband for Karen. They are my friends. Amen."

Before we passed the corn I thought how neat Andy's prayer had been. No one had ever introduced me to God before. In his own childlike way Andy taught me a new way to see God and that's a pretty grown up thing to do.

Way to go, Rooster.

...LLL

The Day the Drugstore Died

My father sat me on the marble counter
near the register of our old drugstore,
   and handed me a cold orange pop.
Another man stood by, smiled, then shook
   my father's hand to complete their deal.

So ended chocolate malts at closing
   shaken to froth in the tiny green machine,
consumed with giggles during family time,
   and followed by another chance
to pick a favorite comic from the rack.

So ended the noisy streets,
   the dirty boys next door,
walks to the ice cream store and school,
   ice men hauling up our stairs,
coal dust on the basement floor.

So began the quiet nights
in large yards waiting to be mowed,
   with neighbors who were all alike
in ties with suits on long commutes
   and all those thieves of time we find
when in our search for peace
   we sometimes sacrifice our lives.

                                  ...SSG

THE ORPHAN PIG

The one eyed girl
The orphan pig
And the boy with the gap-toothed smile
Were singing songs in the barn
During an afternoon rain
And the boy turned to the girl and said
I heard it plain
They was talking down at the mill
Not knowing I knew a word
Or understood
They was saying there was people born
Without imperfections
However that is
As if they got ears
On both sides of their head
Just the same

They call it "Normal" they do
Coldest word I ever heard
And no one said a word against them
Said how pitiful sad
Or remarked that
They Mommas still loved them
Just the same

There's no special schools for them
No Crutches or braces or even—
Well I couldn't hear no more
It was all I could listen to

Saddest thing I ever heard tell of
Imagine having a Momma that wouldn't
Say she loved them the same
Or just as much

My Momma said it lots of times
I heard your Momma say it too
But they Momma don't say it to them
No wonder they point at us
And try to be spiteful mean
Now they shouldn't feel bad
It may be they have imperfections
On the inside of them
And if they can figure them out
They Momma might love them
Just the same

The orphan pig didn't understand
A word they said
But liked it when they hugged her
But mostly when they sang.

…JBM

Lizard

Summer's lizard slides
across the rock, leaving it
barer than before

...SSG

STYLE

He never wrote poetry right
Colored within the lines
Or followed the rules
Grass is green
Sky is blue
That's the way
It's supposed to be
No one is cutting verbal
Didos on this dance floor
Fred and Ginger already did.

                                              …JBM

Alphanumeric Anatomies

Oh, if I were the number 1,
I would have a lot of fun.
Still, I eat another hero.
My profile is the number 0.
I cinch my belt to hide my weight.
I only look like the number 8.
At "Attention!" I stiffen my spine.
I only manage the number 9.
They say "At ease." I'm in a fix.
My butt drops down to a number 6.
But, if I were the number 1,
I would have a lot of fun.

I would like to be a capital I,
But I guess I'm not that sort of guy.
My gut droops over my belt, you see,
So I look more like a capital P.
Say, I would not mind a capital R.
Then I could be an adult film star.
But that's not likely, what's to do?
Nude I look like a capital Q.
So I'll stay dressed because I know
I really am a capital O.

                                                        ...LLL

About Fear

The grey cocoons were spun
on the porch at night.

Awaking and sensing
aliens, beasts, or spiders,

I smashed all
that I could find.

A few survived
my frenzied fear

to become in the end
the small white butterflies

I call friends.

...SSG

LEFTOVERS

Sometimes I feel like leftovers
In the back of the fridge
Now not that homemade
Chili or potato salad
That improves with an overnights lodging

Rather I am that covered culture container
That reveals pastel green or blues
Or even stranger hues

What is the lure of that milk carton
Well past its posted chronological
That one must dive nose-first
Kamikaze style into

The chicken salad with the faint foul tinge
And what of that cheese
Can we give it a little trim

Is there life in that little orphaned petri dish
There's all kinds of guidance in the Torah
About Pork or fauna and flora
But where is the warning
In Deuteronomy
To save us from household economy

...JBM

Our Time

weaned from
Byzantium
we stalk
in ruin
we walk
from room

to room
and doorsill
to doorway.
(we run
a way).

to wander in
Walden
and wait
in unfamiliar
foyer
up-tight guests

   for our

   Zeitgeist.

...SSG

Little Poems One

Stephen Wright,
Even a poem could he write.
Would it not be just fine
Should he rhyme both ends of each line?

David Hasselhoff and Pamela Anderson
Watching the bay in surf, sand or sun.
Running slo-mo in skimpy suits of crimson
Got their viewers' attention and then some.

Don Mattingly
Said to Yogi
When Dwight Gooden came near,
"His reputation preceded him before he got here."

William Harley and the brothers Davidson
Built their motorcycles just for fun.
They never knew their bikes would urge us
To drink cold beer in the town of Sturgis.

...LLL

Description

for Fred K.

I wrote my inmost thoughts
on the newest, whitest
paper I had ever seen.
I painted the contours of myself
in the sharpest, brightest
colors I could wish to use.
But pen and brush lie useless
when nothing's left to say;
and foxing yellows
as color fades away.
Then, that outline of myself--
it too, has gone, with you.

…SSG

MILK 'N CORNBREAD

Once asked
If I was related to Jesse James,
I had to confess that our family names
Had a long difficult history
Establishing all that paperwork,
Let alone biological bona fides.
I might well be related to the Pope
Or some other worthy soul
For all I knew
But it isn't likely

They say there's no disgrace in being poor
The advantages though are notoriously slim
There's homemade biscuits and gravy galore
Even if the soup is a little thin
And long before svelte hollow cheeks were in
Our waistlines were always fashionably trim

We recycled everything
Aluminum foil to wrapping string
And you would be amazed
How far you can stretch a buck
When you only got fifty-four cents
I've never stood before
An open refrigerator door
Overcome with indecision

I can still hear my Momma's voice saying:
"You'll spoil your dinner!"
But it never happened.

            …JBM

Mel Famey

Deuces were wild. The game was tied two to two with two men on base and two outs in the bottom of the ninth when the Muncie Muscats' manager called to the bullpen for his all-star closer.

"Famey! Send in Mel Famey!"

The Forsyth Nine had expected this move. Before the game they placed a keg of ice-cold beer in the Muscats' bullpen. It was a scorcher of a day, but the keg was in a tub of ice and covered with a tarp until the seventh inning stretch when a couple of groundskeepers removed the tarp. Most of the Muscats' pitchers, including Mel Famey, helped themselves to a mug or two. Mel walked out to the mound and took his warm-up tosses. He confidently threw eight consecutive balls walking in the winning run. The Forsyth Nine jubilantly rushed onto the field. Someone hoisted the keg high overhead and led the ball players in a parade. When asked why they were doing this, one of the Forsyth Nine said, "Because that's the beer that made Mel Famey walk us."

...LLL

Chapter Two

I Am the Queen	SSG
Carole's Boxes	SSG
Float Trip	LLL
Fear Pays a Visit	SSG
Little Poems Two	LLL
The Chase	SSG
Parkinson's Song	LLL
History	JBM
Sometimes	SSG
Morning Rituals	JBM
Peggy Lee	SSG
Trial of the One-Eyed King	JBM
Urban Battle	SSG
Rhinoceros	JBM
Billy Blue	SSG
Roy Rogers	LLL

I Am the Queen

The queen sits royally on a box of tin. Looks out at me royally again. She has her ermine cape and crown of gold. Her sash is there and a cross peeks demurely beneath her breast. The Queen does not, does not I say, fully approve. Her eyes suggest a slight disdain to say: "I have just been crowned, why oh why am I on this tin, this tin of toffees--"English favourites" though they may be? Someone's idea of souvenirs. Someone--whose name is Benson, or so the box declares. Someone who somehow thought it sane to celebrate the crowning of a queen with a toffee tin. I am Her Majesty The Queen, it clearly states in gold and even ER is inscribed. I am the second and have been here all these years; the first, you know, had only forty five to do. Doubtful she was ever on a toffee tin. It's hardly fair. Elizabeth Regina, yet here on a red tin I sit staring out in air. Waiting, it would appear for rescue. It will not come, I know that now. It's taken over sixty years. And still I wait and still I try to smile.

...SSG

Carole's Boxes

Last night I opened the last big box. No surprises there. Much of it were things I thought she had forgotten. We always bought things for one another that we ourselves would like. And here they were, traveling fifteen hundred miles back to me again. I've arranged some of them on the dining room table—not the Formica one of my parents which my brother-in-law threatened to send. The necklace I made her is by the gilded egg I created with our photos and birthdates. Then the small ring box with the gold angel and framed mustard seed. My note said to trust the mustard seed and the angel would do the rest. It didn't turn out as either of us hoped. But I have these memories, these proofs that I tried—like the near-by photo of me forming a cross of driftwood over her mid-section as we stood by the ocean. Always, the undercurrent of I know not what. It could be love, it could be blood, it could be karma—some former life that formed the present. Always there's the uncontrollable creation of the urges we can't recognize, that we can't manipulate within ourselves. So these pieces like the driftwood are what I have left. Yes I do have that driftwood somewhere here—maybe on the sunporch. I could bring it in and place it on the dining room table but it's just too late. So I continue to open boxes, continue to build my memorial to something I don't even recognize. I've added cards from her funeral. The candles and decorated Easter eggs were already there along with the stone that says "Hope" and the list we made during her last days of "Why I Love My Sister."

...SSG

FLOAT TRIP

Bickering, Bickering
The children are bickering
Sayeth the Oracle
Of yon Ozark Hills

Taum Sauk, the Oracle,
Sits quietly brooding
O'er the black waters
Of those Ozark Hills

Still, bickering, bickering,
The children come bickering
Far from their homes of
Comfort and ease.
Coming to pause over five gallon buckets,
Coming to slumber in dreary front seats,
Coming together grumbling, rumbling,
And bickering, bickering, bickering, still.

The ILL-EE-noise mom in the East
Is a-stirring,
Stirring, but silent,
Just biding her time.

While in the West
The great snapper is watching
Watching and waiting---
Awaiting the time,

When the parents come
Paddling, paddling, paddling
When the parents come paddling
Each errant behind.

…LLL

Fear pays a visit

Fear rattles the doorknob.
"No one's at home," I say,
as I cower behind the door.
Fear snorts derisively, "You fool,
I know you're there,
I can hear, just open up
and save some time."

The door thumps and I know it's him,
I can tell by the strain on the lock.
Slowly I rise to my toes to peer
through the peephole, but alas,
his wicked eye looks back at me.
Again he snorts derisively, "I see,"
he says, "I see you there."

Suddenly a shadow passes slowly
near the window and then a tap.
"Tap, Tap," he says, laughing lightly,
"Tap, tap, it's only me, just fear--
how many do you know?"
"Too many" I cry, "I don't want more!"
"But this one is real" says he.

Again I shout, louder than before,
"Go away! Go away! For once and for all!"
But then a bloody hand scratches
at the window pane. I think I see
the curtain sway and once again
I cry. This time I really cry.
"You're ruining my life you beast!
Why won't you go away?"
"Silly you," fear says, "I only want
for you to come out and play."

I'm silent now, as I imagine
what games he wants to do.
"Don't you see," says fear,
"That's exactly what I like about you.
It's why I'm banging at your door
and why I come each night.
You have such grand imagination
it makes my juices flow!"

...SSG

Little Poems Two

You fellas Harley and Davidson
Pull your chaps and jackets on
V-twin thunder may be your passion
But you also dictate leather fashion.

When Trigger died,
Roy had him stuffed and brought inside
To the living room which was a little bigger.
That was the last time Roy mounted Trigger.

Oceola? Oseola? Osceloa?
Just a bit to the east of Pensacola,
Spelling your name is truly quite hard.
Why wasn't it changed on Ellis Island
When you got your green card?

Abraham Lincoln, a circuit court rider
Had a mare and was seated astride her.
Said Lincoln, when her foot tangled in his stirrup,
"I'll climb down if you're climbing up."

…LLL

The Chase

for the hunted

Yours are the doe's eyes
   moving in shadows as horses
trample sunlit hills
   that once stretched out green.

Yours is the slender neck
   that pulsates in heartbeats
as they circle with noise
   of harsh hounds and climatic voices.

And that is the neck that runs
   red as they drink deep
of their own exhilaration
   leaving doe's eyes unclosed.

But you at least have been
   pursued while they are
only hunting hills that
   crackle brown behind them.

                                …SSG

A PARKINSON PLACE SONG
FOR VOICE AND DRUM

Tune: More or less the Jets song from *West Side Story adapted by Larry Ladd*

When you're a Park, you're a Park all the way
From your first Sinemet to your last Parkin' day.
When you're a Park, you may freeze. You may fall.
Your meds either work or do nothing at all.
      You're stiff as a bone.
      Your wiring is defective.
      DRUM ^ ^ **(Two strong beats)**
      Your muscles are stone.
      Your neurons aren't protected.
      You're disconnected.
      DRUM ^ ^ ^^ ^ **(Five beats)**

When you're a Park, you're in good company.
Look at Michael J. Fox and Muhammad Ali.
When you're a Park if your future seems grim,
Other Parks understand and you can lean on them.
      You act like a flake.
      Your memory may be shaken. *DRUM* ^ ^
      "Are these pills I need to take? *(speak or sing)*
      Or, ones I should have taken?"
      "Could I be mistaken?" *DRUM* ^ ^ ^^ ^
      Then, your meds flip a switch
      And your synapses start firing, *DRUM* ^ ^
      You move without a hitch
      And not a sign of tiring.
      You are inspiring! *DRUM* ^ ^ ^^ ^

When you're a Park, at the Parkinson Place
You've got family around; there's a smile on your face.
When you're a Park, you can dance in a chair.
You can reach for the clouds. Goals seem reachable there.

When you're a Park **...YOU...STAY...A ...PARK!**

　　　　　　　　　　　　　　　　　　　　...LLL

HISTORY

We are looking at our own reflections
A mirror on our chosen past

Narcissus would have understood
And knowing Greeks I am sure
They knew this all along

It is said you cannot change the past
Nonsense
Rewrite the history books

We've been doing it since
The alphabet was invented.

...JBM

Sometimes

Sometimes your thoughts
come back to me
as the bird wings
in at twilight,
soars, circles,
seems to plummet
then sweeps itself
back up again
chirping me
to wakefulness
and taking flight
into the night
leaving only one
lonely star behind.

...SSG

MORNING RITUALS

I awoke this morning
And found the toothpaste cap
Properly affixed
…..And I remembered he was gone

The bathroom mirror was not streaked
No towels crumpled in the floor
No unnecessary lights left on
…..And I remembered I was alone

No coffee rings on the counter
No toast crumbs in the butter
The jelly jar wiped and put away
…..And I remembered he was dead

The remote control was mine
The morning crossword puzzle too
There was no brooding silence
….Across the table to placate

There was but one thing left to do
…..Dispose of the body

…JBM

Peggy Lee

I.

Peggy,
you were
soft and hard
cool and hot
big car,
little MG
a fantasy
on the sunny
side of the fifties.
When we believed
we could be
everything.

II.

Peggy,
you were
all the
      bleached blonde
      Revlonized
      buxom-bound
      billboard-bred
patented things we saw
      through a mist
     and called
      American
        sex.

III.

Peggy,
your voice
calmed us
stayed level
even in the chaos
of the horns
even in the fever
of our desire.
We had a crush
on you and they
couldn't take
that away from us.

IV.

But Peggy,
after the sixties
you barely smiled
rarely moved
began to close your eyes.
We faded from view.
Now there've been
some changes made.
Everybody's
on a slow boat
to China.
So
is that all there is?

                              ...SSG

TRIAL OF THE ONE-EYED KING

Perhaps like me you have heard it said
That in the land of the blind
The one-eyed man would be king
Before we adopt this proposition
I would caution that we should listen
To the men who give witness
At the trial of the one-eyed man
In the land of the blind

Why just this morning he said
There was a gathering of the forces of nature
He called clouds
Said we were sure to have a rainstorm
Before the day was half past
And of course it did not happen
Why my old aching bones
Are more accurate and true
And we lost a half day's work
Listening to prophecy from him

On a single morning he calls
Two different eggs
Alike to every man here
In all other respects he calls
One the brown and one the white
Now no other man can discern
Any difference between them

Once I asked the color of a leaf
From this very tree
He said it was green
In but days after that
He said it was tinged red
And just days later
He called it yellow
Then in but a fortnight
These self-same leaves he called

Brown and dead
Then in but days after
They fell from that tree
What kind of witchcraft is this?

He has said that blood
And tears of grief
Are not alike
Though there are wise men here
Who would say this is not so
He claims that with a splash or two
Of cool water upon the face
You may remove all trace
Of sorrow from that face
How can this be?

A boulder or fresh fallen limb
That might harm any passing man
Hurling him to the ground
Has no power over him
He visions along the path
And calls forth the name of a man
Who within our midst shortly stands
Yet when he is asked to vision something
He says he cannot because it is night

He does not fear fire!
These are not the gifts
Of a normal man
They are the powers of demon worship
Consort with the devil necromancy!
Is this the wisdom that we should crown?
Rather I say bring him down
Blind this offending eye
Silence this voice
This man must be destroyed
Before others like him
Arise among us.

                                        ...JBM

Urban Battle

As he lay
sleepless
in bed
in a hot
room
in an angry
city
he heard
the helicopter
circle closer.

His legs crouched
his arms
tightened
round the rifle
in his mind.
He waited rigid
until the sound
was loud enough
and fired
and fired again.

On the fourth shot
his heart stopped
and at last
he died
in a not so
imaginary
war.

...SSG

RHINOCEROS

There was a rhinoceros
Lying on the side of the road
Dead as a doornail as near as I could tell
Now it had been wrapped in some sort of plastic or cloth
And the horn appeared to have been sawed off as well
Oletha and I was coming back from the grocery store
And she said
"That's not a rhinoceros, that's a Christmas tree!"
Well Oletha don't know squat
Never seen a dead rhinoceros in her life
Course it was disguised as a Christmas tree
The city picks those up for free
But can you imagine what they would charge
To pick up a dead rhinoceros
Well I drove around the block to take another look
And sure enough
It was a rhinoceros
Disguised as a Christmas tree
Now I know how these things can happen
There ain't nothing in the world
Cute as a baby rhinoceros
Black or White
But you got to have an awful big backyard
To keep one of them penned
They mess up the carpet with their muddy feet
So you got to keep them outside
In the cold and the heat
And just imagine how much they eat
Well you can flush a Goldfish down any toilet bowl
And you can bury a Hamster
In about any small hole
But a dead rhinoceros
That's a whole different can of beans
Is it any wonder they disguise them
As Christmas trees?

                                                    ...JBM

Billy Blue

    Billy Blue drove blue cars
with "Billy Blue" two feet high
    on the outside and Bill Blue
sitting six feet tall inside.

    Country girls and country men
came to country bars to see
    Billy play and dance and roar
his big blond blue-eyed laugh.

    Billy Blue had a bold tattoo
and wore a rolled up sleeve
    to show it off, until he got
a khaki shirt that covered all.

    Then Billy sat in foreign bars
with no one he knew 'til his tattooed
    arm was severed and his blue eyes
were dulled and blond hair was blood.

    Billy Blue was killed
by a dirty khaki war
    and he's not the same hero
he had been anymore.

                                     ...SSG

Roy Rogers

Roy had just bought a new pair of boots that were a sight to behold. They were beautiful. The first thing Roy did when he got them home from the store was to treat them with an oil-based waterproofing agent and hand rub them until the uppers were soft to the touch. Then he set them on the front porch to dry overnight. Roy turned in for the night unaware that a mountain lion was on the prowl. Sometime during the night that cat got a whiff of those boots and was drawn to them. When she got to them, it was like she had fallen into a field of catnip. She wrestled the boots. She tossed the boots. But mostly she chewed on the boots.

Roy was up at dawn. When he stepped onto the porch, he instantly saw his boots – scratched, mauled, chewed, and covered with cat drool. He saddled up, loaded his rifle, and set out to find that cat. The she-lion did not make it easy for Roy, but after trailing her for several long hours, Roy got a shot and ended her days on the prowl. He draped the carcass over his saddle and rode back to the ranch. Dale was waiting for him and he dumped the dead lion on the porch at her feet. Dale looked at Roy with awe and admiration and began to ask the musical question: Pardon me Roy is that the cat that chewed you new shoes?

...LLL

Chapter Three

Rafting	LLL
Black Holes	SSG
Winter	LLL
Mama's Jingle	SSG
Poets in the Room	JBM
The Lonely Hour	SSG
Verklempt	JBM
Ocean View	SSG
Afternoon Trains	SSG
Fortune's Favorite	JBM
Dance with the Dragon	SSG
Little Poems Three	LLL
Wallpaper Redux	JBM
Strawberry	LLL

RAFTING

For years afterwards, we wore t-shirts that boldly proclaimed (with full-color illustration) "ON THE EIGHTH DAY GOD RAFTED". We were out to make a family memory one bright July morning on the Snake River in Jackson Hole, WY. The advertisement for a white water rafting excursion had lured us out of our campground and away from our usual vacation distractions. We were not a particularly athletic bunch, but who needed athleticism to paddle a rubber raft downstream? At the check-in station, we donned our life jackets. The guide instructed us in some basics of river travel. He gave us a lesson in "hydraulics".

"Hydraulics" is an awkward sounding word better suited to a mechanic's toolbox than to the majesty of a mountain river. Simply put, hydraulics is the study of fluids in motion. Applied to a flowing river, hydraulics can be hazardous to your health. When rapidly moving water encounters an obstacle like a boulder or submerged log, turbulence is created. The turbulent water opens an area of lowered pressure behind and below the obstacle, then rushes in to equalize the pressure. For a moment the water flowing downstream reverses its direction and flows upstream with enough force to take branches, canoes and people with it. Our guide stressed this final point. He definitely did not want a hydraulic to carry any of his people away so he went on to instruct us in the rules to follow if we found ourselves outside of the raft for any reason. First, we were to grab the safety rope wrapped around the sides of the raft. If that failed, we were to grab the paddle of one of our crewmates and be pulled back into the raft. Failing that, we were to turn our bodies to face downstream and raise our legs as high as we could so that we were floating feet first until we were through the rapids and could swim ashore or be picked up by a raft. The reason for looking downstream was to see what you were about to hit.

Raising your legs meant your feet might hit first, but it was also intended to prevent a hydraulic from grabbing your dangling feet and pulling you under.

Brimming with this newfound knowledge, I sat high on the sidewall of the raft in the number one oarsman's position. Our first half an hour or so was placid. The breeze was cool on the water and the rhythmic dip-pull-recover of the paddle was relaxing. Our guide joked and kept up a steady stream of naturalists' trivia as we approached our first rapids. Suddenly we were thrown into the rush of the rapids and urged to paddle. The raft began to buck and pitch like a rodeo bull. My right foot was tucked under the sidewall and against the raft floor to anchor my position. I kept a steady pace with my paddle but as I stroked down, the raft raised its head out of the water and my paddle met no resistance. The unexpected nothingness threw my center of gravity out of the raft and demanded that I follow. My right foot pulled free and I let my paddle swim on its own. I grabbed for the safety rope. When the river caught my legs, my fingers tightened on the rope, which turned into a skin-tearing rasp in my grasp. The rope burnt into my flesh. I let go. "Grab a paddle," I thought. I grabbed a paddle only to realize my twelve-year-old son, Michael, was holding the other end. Surely he was more likely to be pulled in than I was to be pulled out. Again, I let go. I immediately lost track of what the raft was doing because I was busy dealing with those pesky hydraulics.

My feet hung down and pulled me under. I held my breath waiting for my life vest to buoy me up. A few seconds passed before I decided to help. I began to swim upward for all I was worth. The water changed from a dark green to a foamy white as I neared the surface. Then, as quickly as throwing a switch, I was plunged back into the dark green. As the river dragged me along, I sensed ever-changing pockets of coldness. At times my legs and torso

seemed to be in different climates. I found this interesting and casually wondered when I would reach the surface. My lungs were demanding air, but my mind was calm. I watched bubbles rising to the surface. I feared that I would crash into submerged rocks, but when I at last reached the surface, I was unharmed. Gasping for breath, I looked for the raft. It was 100 yards upstream. The current was still carrying me away from the raft, but I managed to give the "thumbs up" sign. I heard a voice shout, "There he is!" I was too busy trying to catch my breath to answer. Devouring large chunks of air, I turned to face downstream and raised my feet.

Waiting for the raft to overtake me, I was thankful to see the bright blue sky that July day on the Snake River in Jackson Hole, WY. I no longer think of brake fluid and actuator valves when I hear the word "hydraulics." Now I envision underwater snags and swirling water momentarily rolling upstream dragging what it can with it. Our souvenir t-shirts have long since worn out and been discarded, but the day dad fell out of the raft still lives vividly in our family's memory.

...LLL

Where are black holes when you need them?

For billions of years
I've been turning.
Spinning some would say.
Believe me,
it's more like turning.

Everyday there's Venus,
every night the moon.
Every year they're digging
every spring they've grown.

Yet I am going nowhere,
always with that burning
in the belly longing
for that one black hole.

So often life
is tedious, I wish
that it were gone.
If only some idiot
had not invented dawn.

...SSG

Winter

Winter's bony fingered hand
Tightly grips the sullen land.

Stinging sleet,
Slippery feet,

Salty puddles of melting snow.
Careful now take it slow.

Unexpected frantic dance
I sit down hard
And wet my pants.

...LLL

Mama's Jingle

Marijuana
   Marihuana
is the devil's
   dingle-dangle
used by mesmerizers
   who mislead
our honest youth.

Marijuana,
   Mariguana
is the soft underbelly
   we pull in
full of that Satan
   we must cast out.

...SSG

POETS IN THE ROOM

Speak softly, speak softly
There are poets in the room
With tender ears that hear dissonance
Faint as pin's fall on broadloom
Or broken meter harsh as silent Cygnet swans
Drifting by

Speak softly, speak softly
Lest the poets flee the room
To claw and scrawl on vellum
Well rooted metaphor
And spelling created anew
With quills of slurry ink
Leaving black blood trails of passion

Speak softly, speak softly
For poets need their sleep
To dream in perfect couplets
With every eyelid's flicker
All the words lost to rude alarm clocks
And awakening yawns

...JBM

The lonely hour

You've turned your back to me.
The geese are far away.
The sun has yet to rise.

It is the lonely hour.
When for company,
I turn to whistling
trains and selves
of former lives.

...SSG

VERKLEMPT

A fog fell over the backyard fence
Crept across the grass
Covered the empty sandbox
Where once a child had laughed
Clouded the foot of the sliding board
Climbed a tree house ladder
Rung by rung
And hid the swing set seat
Where once a child had sung
Higher Daddy Higher
And touched the stars
With barefoot toes

A Mother and Father have long since left
Along with the promises they once kept
…"For richer or poorer, in sickness and health,
Until death do us part…"

The Sun will rise soon and burn the traces away
Leaving a million dewdrop tears
To rust the chains that once held the world together
For a child who touched the stars
With barefoot toes while singing
Higher Daddy Higher.

…JBM

Ocean View

Tiny fluorescent creatures
float within my veins.
Ancient giant turtles
paddle in my brain.
My hermit crab is floating
near my sea anemone.
Plus I think there's coral
building a shelf for all to see.

These days it seems
more tide arrives than leaves,
so many tide pools stay
deep inside of me.
It won't be long before
the levee starts to crack
and floods of poems rush
through my sterile streets.

...SSG

Afternoon Trains

There were
fine plump pillows
on the afternoon train.
I doubt that I
shall see them again.

Some cars
had windows lined
with lace although
I doubt that there will be
such in this place.

I've imagined
all this for me and
for you as writing of
pillows, trains and lace
was all there was to do.

...SSG

FORTUNE'S FAVORITE

Mama made Hard-luck soup
Said it was Miss Fortune's favorite
Whenever this guest of honor arrived

Cast iron kettle and lots of broth
Blessed with regrets, woe-is-me
And a little fat-back

Somehow we muddled through
When barely enough was enough
With no pushing and shoving
To get into the lifeboat

That was the way we chose to remember
Our close call brushes with disaster
The smoke and mirrors of pious platitudes
Endless clichés and the unanswered prayers

A trail of broken promises
Prolific as stars and constellations wide.

...JBM

Dance with the Dragon

Dragons dance with firecracker tails.
Black eyed peas bubble on the stove.
A ram's horn echoes over the hills.
And someone lets down the goat.
Others drop a great moon pie,
and even Snooki gets put in a ball.

Some houses get cleaned.
Some can't be swept at all.

Whether we do or don't

Always

We honor the sun
honor the moon
render to Caesar
or honor a pope

We must be grateful for time

So we

Dance and blow and drop
and the date doesn't matter
nor what we blow or drop
nor where-- because after all
every day's a new year

even today

           …SSG

Little Poems Three

Zen cognoscente David Carradine,
Master of koan, what does this mean?
If I sell a poem written in free verse,
Is it still free verse?

Master of koan Chuck Norris,
What does this mean?
If a tetanus shot with a rusty needle I got,
Would I need another tetanus shot?

Bruce Lee master of koan,
What does this mean?
If a goldfish swims hard into the side of it bowl,
Do tears fill its eyes and overflow?

To Archibald MacLeish
"A poem should not mean, but be."
Yet, in its being,
Should it not have meaning?
Hey! Why don't the first two lines rhyme?
Say, is this another one of those koan things?

            …LLL

WALLPAPER REDUX
(TIMES WAS HARD)

When I was a boy we were so poor
We even had to rent wallpaper
Hung with tacks so we could take it back
When Momma wanted to redecorate

No one in our family was overweight
Or ever pushed back a half-filled plate
Hard work, long hours, damn little luck
Pinching our pennies stretching a buck

Some pick themselves up by their bootstraps
Only first you got to have some boots
And we ate them a long time ago
For years I thought a toothpick was dessert

Daddy would give you a nickel if you skipped a meal
Then in the middle of the night would replace it with a
dog's tooth
(Told us the Tooth Fairy came by drunk)
Where do you suppose he ever got a fool idea like that
I remember one year we ate the Christmas tree for Thanksgiving

Another year for Thanksgiving
Momma baked a potato for us
And we all got stuffed just like rich folks
She even forgot the cranberries.

                                              ...JBM

Strawberry

Once a strawberry farmer put just the right amount of this and that in his strawberry patch and produced a single strawberry as big as his head. He was very proud of its beauty, but he also recognized its monetary value. Seed companies would pay a pretty penny to get their hands on this berry. He called his insurance company and asked for an appraiser to come by and give him an estimate. In a little while a man showed up and asked to see the berry. Assuming this was the appraiser, the farmer led him to the berry. As soon as he saw the berry, the man grabbed it up and began to run. "Wait!" shouted the farmer, aren't you here to appraise my berry?" The berry thief shouted over his shoulder, "I came to seize your berry, not appraise it!"

...LLL

Chapter Four

Asher	LLL
Sub-Urbia	SSG
Sharon's Theory	SSG
Beauty	JBM
Verses From Vesuvius	SSG
Song of the Sailor	LLL
Picque-Nique	JBM
The Crabapple Tree	SSG
Lost Horizons	SSG
Little Poems Four	LLL
Touché Cliché	JBM
Secret Dissenters	SSG
Bird Bordello	JBM
Pavement	LLL

ASHER

Our lives, and the people we become, are shaped by the people we meet along the way. Well, not just meet along the way, but the people we pay attention to and the things we remember about our encounters with them.

In the early 1950s we began a series of family vacations that took us to Lake Gladstone just north of Brainerd, Minnesota. My family went there every summer for about ten years. Dad first drove us there in a maroon 1949 Mercury with overdrive and a backseat large enough to contain three "Here's-the-line-on-the-seat-don't-cross-it" children. Dad never had to say, "Don't make me pull over." We behaved ourselves as dad drove the 721 miles from St. Louis to Lake Gladstone. We were up at 3:30AM to get an early start. We drove it in one day so as not to waste any fishing days. I am still in awe of my dad's stamina in being able to pack the car, drive 721 miles, unpack the car, set up housekeeping, and be in a fishing boat at dawn the next day.

Still, he wasn't the only one. Don, a hardware store manager from Peoria, Illinois, was equally dedicated. Dawn would find him in the boat with dad. Don's son, Bobby, was a year or so younger than I, but we got along just fine. Most days would find us playing some variant of war. We loved to form hand grenades from the sandy mud around the lakeshore and leave them overnight to dry just enough to hold together. Then we would begin our assault on the enemy position lobbing hand grenades at the imagined foe. When the sandy-dirt, semidry clods hit the ground, they would splatter and create a plume suggesting an explosion. Between war and a variety of things we could do with our hunting knives, pocketknives, and assorted pieces of Cub Scout gear, we stayed occupied.

The resort was a family business operated and owned by Asher and Jesse Neimala – a "Yah – you betcha -- for sure" couple of Scandinavian heritage. Asher worked at the sawmill in Brainerd; Jesse worked at the resort. In 1952 Asher and Jesse had a duplex and a single cabin. They lived in half of the duplex and rented the other half and the single. By 1962 they had six or eight units.

My first memory of Asher revolved around the stripping of some birch trees. Bobby and I had been to the gift shops in Nisswa, the nearest town, and had seen the small birch bark canoes offered as Native American crafts. We had our knives and some idea that if we gathered the birch bark, we could fashion our own canoes. So we set out one afternoon to peel bark from some of the trees. We stood between four and five feet tall. Our incisions were made between chest and eye level. We cut into the flesh of the trees and skinned them in neat bands, which immediately caught Asher's eye when he got home from work. He was furious!

Fortunately for Bobby and me, Asher talked to our parents before he talked to us. By the time Bobby and I stood before him he was calm. The adults had agreed on a plan. Asher began with a lesson in forestry. He carefully explained that the trees might die from such an attack as we had made. Even if they lived, there would be a permanent scar around each trunk. We apologized and promised never to cut a living tree again. But, (and this was the kind of guy Asher was) he took us to a brush pile in the woods near where they split logs for the winter. He told us we could help ourselves to any log or bark that we might need for one thing or another. Then the final part of our planned punishment was revealed. We had to go with Asher to pick up the trash around the resort, load it in his truck, and go with him to dump it.

The indignity! The treachery! Our parents had agreed to this child labor scheme. How could they do this? Didn't they know we had ammunition to manufacture and bunkers to assault? The futility of presenting our objections was clear to us. We had been sold down the river before we could mount a defense. Not to mention the fact that we were so painfully, obviously guilty as charged.

Asher took us to the shed/garage/workshop that housed everything he needed to keep the resort running. He searched through a few boxes of rusting hinges, pliers, and those old fashion wrenches that once came with new cars and tractors. Finally, he came up with two right handed and two left handed gloves. It didn't seem to matter to Asher whether the size, type, or manufacturer matched up. I suspect he figured the garbage wouldn't know the difference. Asher pulled a pair of once yellow now mostly oily black gloves from his hip pocket and put them on.

"You boys start with those boxes."

He pointed to a pile of wooden boxes filled with trash. Then he did something that astounded Bobby and me. He bent down and picked up a fifty-five gallon drum full of trash and set it in the truck bed as easily as setting a can of soup on the pantry shelf. Now, Asher was not a big man. In fact, my father at five feet nine inches stood half a head taller than Asher, but he was about as strong a man as I have ever seen. The truck was soon filled with drums and boxes. We were off to the dump.

Bobby and I, still embarrassed by our crime, sat in silence. On the way to the dump, we left the dirt road and turned onto a concrete highway. We were soon chugging across the county in a somewhat dilapidated, red pickup truck that looked like it was made for hauling trash. We passed a field and Asher honked and waved at the farmer on his tractor. Curious, I asked, "Who was that?"

"I don't know," he said.

"But you honked and waved at him," I protested.

"You betchca."

Asher had a serious look on his face. As serious as when he told us of the fate of the trees. He continued:

"Now that man saw a red pickup truck whose driver honked and waved. When he goes in tonight, he's going to say to his wife that he thinks he saw his cousin Richie, or maybe Bob Hearns from over at Gillam. He'll say a man and maybe a couple of kids were in the truck. Richie's got a red pickup. Bob's pickup is more orange than red, but he has two boys. He'll say he studied on it all afternoon and he thinks they should call the Hearns and see how they are doing. And he may remember that he still has cousin Richie's chain saw that he borrowed last spring. He and his wife will have a good talk about folks who have red pickup trucks."

He paused. "Do you understand?"

We didn't understand at all, but we nodded.

Asher's face lost its serious expression and softened into a smile. He began to sing, "Row, row, row your boat gently down the stream," at the top of his voice. Pretty soon all three of us were singing "Row, row, row your boat" in an off-key, ragged round, which did not end until we got to the dump.

Our punishment had a lasting impact on me. I never looked at a stranger the same way again. Going to the dump with Asher became a highlight of our vacations. That was over fifty years ago, but every now and then, when I drive past a lone farmer in his field, I honk the horn and wave.

...LLL

Sub-Urbia

    Quiet, peaceful, land of rolling greens,
friendly surroundings, stacked with magazines.
    Low, sleek--on with the trend;
put up some fences end to end.

Breathe!
    Breathe the trees
    Breathe the sky
    Breathe the cabbage smell
        and can't you just taste
        that barbeque as well.

Twelve hundred a month, with a fistful of seed.

Listen!
    Listen to the gale
    Listen to the peace
    Listen to the wail
        the pounding sound
        of your own heart.

Twelve hundred a month, with a fistful of seed.

On the left, a wood thrush sang.
Bang!
On the right, a trumpet blows.
Do? Re? Mi? ...Do? Re? Me?

Boom-Crack! Boom-Crack!
a hammer breaks through the shell.
Ba-Room! a truck goes by.
Fissst! Watch the dust fly.

Come down from your cloud
and watch your dreams being plowed.

Watch!
Watch the sun,
(but not too close)
Watch the cars,
Watch the flowers,
Watch your neighbor's niece,
Watch the stars
(but not too long).

Sit on your padded patio,
and watch your life's lease run out.

All, only twelve hundred a month
and a fistful of seed.

...SSG

Sharon's theory of the origin of the universe.

I have quarked my way through the universe
and not just in my dreams.
I've rattled protons with every step
and you have done the same.
Neutrons slosh round our feet.
Electrons bounce from chin to shin.
Black holes creep toward us then retreat.
Light flutters around our head like butterflies
with particles of red and blue turned purple
in the fiery furnace of our alchemy.

We, you and me, are the center of the universe
and anyone who tells you otherwise
simply postulates the wrong hypotheses.

...SSG

BEAUTY

"Scarlett O'Hara was not beautiful, but men seldom noticed..."

Anyone can be beautiful
That's an accident of birth

Anyone can be charming
That's a gift of tongue

But to have je ne sais quoi
That is a real art

Je ne sais quoi
Something unexplained

Je ne sais quoi
Something never named

An aura or glow
That certain certain-light

That dances across the room
To make candle flames blush

And turns vin ordinaire into
The Thorn in the Flesh

...JBM

Verses from Vesuvius

    Every baby born was turned to stone.
Meals prepared at noon still wait for spoons.
    This solid arm that reached out for love
embraced eternal time instead.

    And thus they wait the brush of eyes
to touch their face, the quickened breath
    that often comes when fissures whisper
of common frailty in uncommon stone.

                                                   ...SSG

Song of the Sailor

I love to go out sailing on any weekend morn.
I love to get there early before the break of dawn.
I rummage through the ads and plot my course just so.
I grab my cup of coffee, my purse, and off I go.

They blink at me with bleary eyes when I ring their bell.
I say I'd like to see their wares and they say, "Go to Hell."
I start to cry a little and then I start my spiel.
If I stay calm and play it cool, I can clinch this deal.

"I know your ad said 8:00 to 3:00 and I'm early by a hair,
But when you've heard my story I'm certain you will care.
At nine o'clock, I see the doc to get his diagnosis.
I worry every night and day about some grim prognosis."

First a fire took all our stuff, but we started to rebuild.
Next came a flood oozing mud 'til every room was filled.
So, I haggle over price and struggle to make ends meet.
I'd rather be here early than living on the street."

They say, "Now there. We care." The door opens to me.
Their protests mute they lead me to their total inventory.
I chuckle to myself to think that they believed my story.
(I am a modern pirate embracing a landscaped sea.)

There is so much to see -- the priceless and the worthless.
I stand unmoved, stone-faced, pretending to be mirthless.
Whatever treasure I find, whatever price they're asking,
My face stays a total blank, my feelings I'll be masking.

I'm sure that I can turn a buck if I get them down a little.
So I say eight they say ten and we meet in the middle.
I stuff my swag in a paper bag or haul it away in a truck.
I am a yard sale sailor and today I've had good luck.

My plans are charted for today. My sails are full of wind.
Though ladened carports call to me to heave-to and put in,
I must away for another day when the wind is wailing.
We'll sail that day; we'll sail away – we will go a sale-ing.

…LLL

PIQUE-NIQUE (FRENCH 1826)

Why do we insist on the picnics?
Potato salad and deviled eggs
Out in the wild miles away
From the nearest medical attention

All that mayonnaise and cold fried chicken
Sodium laden chips and pickles
Barbecue and sour cream ranch dips
With salsa on the side

How many have gulled themselves
With thoughts of indigestion
While the salmonella spawns wild
Among the streams of E. coli?

Our little ptomaine trips to commune with Mother Nature.
Out in the blazing sun greased with sun block, toxic insect repellent,
(At least to the bugs but harmless to our more robust constitutions)
charcoal lighter fumes,
Outdoor plumbing in those wretched plastic saunas
With no hand washing facilities
While the city-born children troll the lakes edges
Scouring for poison ivy, oak or poisonous snakes.

Do you think it could be repressed thoughts of revenge?
That so motivates our every Fourth of July binge
When we encourage a few caution reducing frosty cold brews
Before men handle that fireworks display in the dark?

In the eighteenth and nineteenth century
People had their picnics in cemeteries;
Appropriate don't you think?

...JBM

The Crabapple Tree

The crabapple tree
broke my heart today,
trying to run
away with the wind.
Its shattered trunk
reminded me
I am not God,
so many things
I cannot mend.

...SSG

Lost Horizons

We always lived
in tiny houses
with views of fields
and far horizons.

I'm living now
in luxury
hidden by walls
and banks of flowers.

No sunsets here
nor sunrises
the sun is simply
there or gone.

Sometimes in the shadows
I shudder and want
a small home
with clear horizons.

...SSG

Little Poems Four

Juan Ponce de Leon
Searched for a youth giving fountain.
In the Florida grass crouched a lion
Juan's search ended with the pounce de lion.

Teddy's Rough Riders at San Juan
Did not have their horses to ride upon.
They ran when they charged the enemy gunners.
So, why aren't they called Teddy's Rough Runners?

Gambler and gunman Doc Holliday
Said, "Come to Tombstone for a week or a day.
You will find the hotel is truly 1-A,
But I'm afraid the corral is only O.K."

Far Side cartoonist, Gary Larson (larsoon)*
Drew a cowtoon*
Just a simple cow - down to earth,
Then he milked it for all it was worth.

…LLL

Explanatory note: In Cow, Larson, Larsoon, cartoon and cowtoon are all rhymes or near rhymes; or so I'm told – I don't actually speak Cow myself.

Touché Cliché

Lady Cliché
Once a clever turn of phrase
The lingua franca of another age
Elegant as any debutante

But the parties went on much too long
Her steps grew unsteady
Her voice too loud
Gone was the beauty
Once so proud
She stumbled from the literary page
Into the mouths --
Of common usage

Lady Cliché
The makeup gaudy
The eyeliner streaked
No longer is she asked to speak

For all her words
Have been heard before
In softer sibilant tones
But still she prattles on
Witty as always
The last to know
No one is listening

...JBM

The Secret Dissenters

The secret dissenters
sit and scribble
on the undersides
of plastic desks.

They evidence
on restroom walls
in mirror messages
of Ivory soap;

because one-tenth
of them sit pure
in central parks and sing
songs of discontent.

God is alive and unhappy
in upstate New York,
Burbank, Detroit and
Philadelphia, PA.

Stand them up
and count him in
between the lines
as you scribble.

...SSG

BIRD BORDELLO

My next door neighbor
An amiable fellow
Has built a backyard bird bordello
Or a home for unwed avian mothers
Hard to tell which
I don't care I have an open mind
But we have respectable hours
Property values to consider
Not to mention examples
To set for the children

Now he may think
I don't know what's going on
But I wasn't born yesterday
And I watch them all the time
The boyfriends come dragging in
All pimped out in gaudy feathers
All hours of the morning
Whistling and singing
Those bawdy barroom ditties

It's the nestlings
I worry about
Growing up unsupervised
Their mommas work all day
To bring home a little grub

While the daddies are floating
From one fair wind to another
Preening their feathers
And puffing out their chest
Drifting from one perch today
To some handout feeder the next
Splashing in some muddy puddle
Crapping on just washed cars
Hanging toes round the
Birdbath bars

I'm sure my neighbor is a moral fellow
Never bores with some litany of ills
Mows his lawn and pays his bills
But at the drop of a feather
He will wax poetic about Waxwings
Or some Twit's birdsong
He goes on and on
One pollinates, one's a flycatcher
But who wants a bird brothel
For a next door neighbor?

...JBM

Pavement

Once there was a roadhouse where roads came to unwind. Some were footsore at the end of the week. Others were just plain tired. Most were common streets and alleys kicking back with a brew and not looking for trouble. (Oh there were a few nature trails in the back room sipping wine and reading poetry, but no one paid them any mind.) One night, a piece of pavement walked into the roadhouse, glared at everyone and said, "I'm a piece of macadam. I'm tough enough to take you all on at once." No one responded. Another piece of pavement came in and said, "I'm fully cured concrete with steel rods in my spine. I can take you one at a time or all at once." The first piece of pavement rose to the challenge. As the two squared off, the door slammed open and a piece of narrow blue pavement stepped over the threshold. He said nothing, but the first two somewhat sheepishly gave him a wide berth and moved to the bar. One of them said to the bartender, "Don't mess with that guy; he's a cycle path.

...LLL

Chapter Five

Asher II	LLL
Mr. Frost's Cat	SSG
Thought or Prayer	JBM
Silent Lilacs	SSG
Winter's Midnight Trees	SSG
Peach	LLL
Lesson in Humility	SSG
Bedpan Fans	JBM
Ad Infinitum	SSG
Standing Orders	JBM
Have Done So Much	SSG
Little Poems Five	LLL
Trompe L'oeil	JBM
Scapegoat	LLL

ASHER II: REPAIR IT OR PART IT OUT

A telephone joke of the 1950s was to call the corner store and ask the clerk, "Do you have Prince Albert in a can?" When the clerk replied, "Yes," the jokester would say, "Well, let him out!" and hang up. The joke was not all that funny, but prepubescent boys found it hilarious.

Children of the fifties had one eye trained on a prosperous future, one eye on their parents having come through the Great Depression, and one eye looking over a shoulder for the ever threatened mushroom cloud of the Red Menace. Later generations would enter a world that glorified disposability over the 1940s and 1950s credo of "make it do." Kids who grew up with disposable cameras, lighters, razors, telephones, or anything that was more convenient to replace than repair had to reinvent conservation as "ecology" and rediscover saving as "recycling." Post World War II America found many military trained radiomen back in civilian life at a time when the television industry was booming. There were opportunities for television repair services across the country. When personal computers became available a few decades later, there was less advice to "repair" and more advice to "up-grade," which always seems to imply something was being disposed of. In the fifties there was a sense of pride in repairing.

My father had a five horsepower Wizard outboard motor, which was the Western Auto store brand for the Mercury engine. It wasn't fast, but Lake Gladstone wasn't a big lake. It served its purpose and was a faithful companion on many a fishing trip. I can only recall it failing one time. We were heading in for the day when inexplicably the engine sputtered and stopped. Unable to restart it, we had to hitchhike a tow back to the dock.

The engine would not budge when the recoil starter was pulled. We pulled the motor from the boat and took it to Asher's workshed where he had built an engine stand complete with fifty-five gallon drums of water to feed the water pumps while the engines were being tuned. Dad and Asher quickly determined that the water pump had failed, the engine had overheated, and the piston had seized in the cylinder. This was a job for a professional.

The next morning we were cruising the back streets of Brainerd looking for the repair shop Asher had recommended. The proprietor/mechanic looked up from his work long enough to ask, "What can I do for you?" Dad explained the problem and the repairman said, "Let's have a look." I suspected this man and Asher were related or at least had the same interior decorator. Their shops were alike right down to the patina of rust and dust in the corners. This shop smelled like two-stroke engine oil and gasoline.

With the practiced touch of a man familiar with machines, the mechanic confirmed that the water pump's impeller had failed. He then pulled the head and set it aside to expose the piston frozen in the cylinder. "We'll know in a minute whether this is repairable or scrap," he said. Making sure the engine was securely mounted and out of gear, he squirted penetrating oil into the cylinder and waited for it to work. Penetrating oil is special slippery oil made to smell horrible so that mechanics will not confuse it with regular motor oil. This must have been super slippery because it reeked. He picked up a block of wood about the size of a 4x4, or a bit smaller, and a mallet. Placing one end of the block flat on the piston, he brought the mallet down as hard as he could. The piston moved slightly. He applied more penetrating oil and repeated the mallet trick until the piston was free. He concluded the engine was probably repairable. The question never arose as to whether it would be better to buy a new motor. We had the Wizard repaired.

On Lake Gladstone while waiting for the outboard to be repaired, we took turns rowing. Dad recalled when he was in high school he lived on a lake. He would get up early and row across the lake. While he rowed he trolled a spoon (a polished metal fishing lure which resembles a table spoon) behind the boat. He would catch a largemouth bass or a northern pike on the trip over and/or the trip back. So, we trolled until we got the Wizard back.

Sometime later Dad came up with a 1.7 horsepower Neptune trolling motor, which resembled the outboard motor designs of the 1920s and 1930s. The gas tank was mounted on top nestled against the flywheel. The spark plug and cooling fins were exposed. The throttle was a lever, which slid across the front of the engine. The steering lever had no function except to steer. It was a primitive little engine, but it trolled nicely until it shuddered to a stop.

We took the Neptune to Asher's work shed. I was all in favor of taking the head off and hitting it with a mallet. Cooler heads prevailed. Since the flywheel turned freely, the piston had not seized. A bit of dismantling revealed the true culprit. The reed had broken. Several phone calls later, it became apparent that none of the shops in the area dealt the Neptune brand or carried parts that could be substituted. The solution was simple; we would manufacture a reed.

A two-stroke engine reed is akin to the reed in a clarinet or oboe, but it functions more like a one-way trap door to let fuel in and exhaust out. The two-stroke does not use valves; it uses ports to allow fuel into the cylinder and to expel exhaust gases. As the piston moves in the cylinder different ports are exposed or covered. The reed controls the flow of the gases. Reeds are made of spring steel and designed to open one way only and close in the opposite direction.

Dad and Asher set about looking for something from which to make a reed. After a couple of false starts, they came upon a discarded Prince Albert tobacco can. The blue metal was a little thicker than the original reed, but it might work. Dad took tin snips and cut the side panel from the can. He sanded the paint off and laid out his pattern using the broken reed as a template. The tedious work of drilling and filing the piece to completion began and Asher started a story:

"Last winter we had a storm that came on sudden like. I drove to work in the morning under a clear sky with only three or four inches of snow on the ground. When I left work that evening, it had been snowing and the wind had picked up. The highway was in pretty good shape. Between the snowplows and the wind, the road was mostly clear. But when I got to Nisswa and turned off the highway, I had to cut my speed down to a crawl. When I got to the Lake Huber post office and Mercantile I stopped to call Jesse. She said she thought I could make it home. Just before dark she noticed that the wind had blown the snow off the lake. If I couldn't get through in the pick-up, maybe I could walk the last mile or so across the lake. Jesse said while I was at the Mercantile I should pick up a few things: milk, eggs, bread, sugar, and butter. I got our supplies and headed back out into the blizzardy night. I drove at a snail's pace kind of feeling my way along more sensing than seeing where I needed to turn. My windshield wipers were smearing ice on the windshield. In some spots the truck shuddered as the drifts reached the floorboards. I was on the backside of the lake and could see the lights from our house when the pickup slid off the dirt road into a shallow ditch. Jesse had been right about the wind clearing the frozen lake; so, I set out to walk home. But first I remembered to stuff the groceries into the deep pockets of my parka. The wind was cold at my back as I trudged across the lake. I was just happy I didn't have to walk into it. The first part of the crossing was fairly easy, but when I got to our side of the lake there was a problem I had not anticipated. The wind had indeed cleared the lake of snow, but it had deposited the drift where the shoreline rose up to become the yard of our house. The last hundred yards were deeply drifted, but I was committed. I waded in. Soon I was knee deep, thigh deep, waist deep, chest deep in the drift. The snow pressed against me and fought every step I made. I was swimming through the drift using my arms like snowplows to divide the snow in front of me and push it behind me. My progress was slow. My nose was as cold as a pump handle. My fingers were long passed numb. I struggled to keep my footing. Finally, I got high enough up the bank that the snow let me go. I was overjoyed to walk across our yard and get inside. Jesse gave me a hug. I pulled off my gloves and hat and stomped the snow off my boots. Jesse asked me if I had forgotten the groceries. I reached into my parka's pockets to show her I had remembered. The eggs were smashed. The bread was mangled. The cardboard milk carton was leaking at the corners where it wasn't frozen. The sugar bag had burst. The butter was a flattened lump. The milk, bread and eggs were in one pocket; the sugar and butter in the other. I went into the kitchen and scooped the remains of the groceries out of my pockets into a large mixing bowl. As I warmed up by the kitchen stove, I fished the eggshells and wrapping paper out of the bowl. The storm continued to blow outside when Jesse and I sat down to dine on the best French toast we had ever eaten."

Asher smiled, got up, and went over to inspect Dad's work. After a while they agreed that the reed was as good as it was going to be. They installed it and reassembled the Neptune. They started it and it ran. Credit was due to the original designer and manufacturer for not building a disposable product, to Dad and Asher for their ingenuity, and to Prince Albert. I often think of the Neptune repair when I'm faced with a repair project of my own, but it's getting harder to find Prince Albert in a can.

…LLL

Mr. Frost's Cat

(why the Cheshire cat smiles)

The cat sits
on its toes
and knows.
In its bones
are written tomes
of endless memories.

…SSG

THOUGHT OR PRAYER

Soon I shall awaken
From this dowdy brittle chrysalis
Called life
Into flowing white robes
And iridescent wings of gold
To play leapfrog among the clouds
I shall have a singing voice
Of no less than eight octaves
Harpo's gift with strings
I'll even have a built in reading light

Unless of course
Shakespeare's gloomy Dane was right

"The rest is silence"

I wonder if I'll know.

Remember George Bernard Shaw once opined
"In Heaven an Angel is nobody special"

            ...JBM

Silent Lilacs

    silent
            lilacs
                  fall

    on damp ground
            with other growth

        fragrance

            stays behind.

                        ...SSG

Winter's Midnight Trees

Winter's midnight trees
while reaching for summer sun
find beauty in moon.

...SSG

THE PEACH

To those who say,
"There is no God."
I say,
"Eat a peach."

When the first sweet-tart
Sunbright harmony of flavors
Washes the palate,

I defy you
To deny you
Believe.

No God!
Posh!
Else how explain the peach?

...LLL

Lesson in humility

Willows bend to wind.
Water flows to larger seas.
We all have our place.

...SSG

BEDPAN FANS

Stop and think of all those movie stars
In hospitals

After:
Their fourth bypass
Or liver transplant

Meeting:
Another fifty year-old nurse

Who says':
My Daddy was a big fan.

...JBM

Ad Infinitum

As life becomes
a chain of my constructions;
so death is but
a chain of my definings.

...SSG

STANDING ORDERS

Listen soldier
They do not give purple hearts for grief
Tear the cloth gnash teeth
Cover the face with ashes
Another young man has taken
A single step into the shadows
And there fallen

He should have been born
Of a wretched and withered frame
To carry such cruel devastation to our eyes

What second fruit from Eden's garden
Was tasted
That warrants this unholy grace
Of a heart that can
So desolate feel

Grief is the enigmatic pain
Not of bristle and scald
But of the wind
Sucked from every breath

A heart broken but still we live
Surely that broken portion
Must be some place other
That scars more slowly
Than glaciers advance
And shears as precipitously
Into roaring mountains of ice
Haunting our oceans of night

...JBM

Have Done So Much

Have done so much
with so little-
in a quiet place
me and my memory.

Have traveled so far
with an empty suitcase
closed on the floor
and I on my bed.

Have felt so very much
with only a cigarette
and the clinking of ice
in the dark with windows.

When the wind moans
just a little at the corners
and a trumpet with drums
slides through my radio--

I must have danced
a thousand dances
in the crowded rooms
of my memory.

...SSG

Little Poems Five

Senator Fred Thompson said of the political dance,
"If I can't dazzle them with brilliance,
As for position I jockey,
I can always baffle them with a bit of bull hockey.

Mickey Rooney
Short, but not puny
Had nine wives (or maybe eight)
Hated marriage, but loved wedding cake.

Said Mick "Crocodile" Dundee
From the land of the Aborigine,
"I thought I'd forgot 'ow to throw me boomie,
But it came back to me."

Benjamin Spock
The sixties baby doctor
Taught us parenting crafts
Like keeping children out of drafts.

Sarah Palin
Feared her ticket was failing.
So she called Lloyds of London to see
If she could buy a foreign policy.

...LLL

TROMPE L'OEIL

A mirror shatters into a thousand reflections
Each one
A piercing shard
You cannot hold
A mirror shatters into a thousand reflections
Each one
A piece of her
And none of them the whole
A memory shatters into a thousand reflections
Each one
A piece of shard
And none of them the whole
A young soldier has stepped into a mirror
Each one
Pierced with shard
And none of them ever whole
A soldier boy becomes a silhouette
Each one
A piece of heart
Never again to be whole
A mirror shatters into a thousand reflections

...JBM

Scapegoat

The scapegoat was an animal ritualistically designated to take upon itself the sins of a community. Hebrew priests would carefully prepare the beast (Rari, in Aramaic) then lead it into the wilderness with the intent of pushing it over a cliff allowing it and the sins it carried to die. On some occasions the Rari was honored by being allowed to ride in a two wheeled cart. At such a time it is said that as the priests had positioned the cart on the edge of a cliff and were raising the front of the cart to dump the scapegoat out, he looked at them with a tearful eye and, in the manner of Balaam's ass, said, "That's a long way to tip a Rari!"

...LLL

Chapter Six

Asher III	LLL
Daisies Are Fine Company	SSG
Taps Plus One	LLL
Flying Potatoes	JBM
Song to Myself	SSG
The Autopsy	SSG
Little Poems Six	LLL
To a Texas Pothole	JBM
Barren Tree	SSG
Cranes	SSG
Celibate	JBM
Love Is Relative	SSG
Divine Circumspection	SSG
HODAR Salute	LLL
Schmaltz	JBM
Benny	LLL

ASHER III – THE LEAKIN' LENA

Asher's boat dock was very much like his work shed. It appeared to have grown like Topsy, but there was a system to it. Every cabin had a 12-foot, aluminum, v-hull fishing boat assigned to it. The boats and slips at the dock were numbered to match the cabin numbers. Green oars were issued with each boat and the guest was expected to see that these were neither lost nor stolen.

To that end, each boat was emptied at night except for the motors. Motors were chained to the stern and the chains were locked. The external gas tanks could be left in place or taken to the cabins depending on how skittish the crowd seemed to be at the time. During periods of national unrest like the Bay of Pigs fiasco or when Russian sent troops into Hungary, most folks kept their gas tanks with them. During quieter times the gas tanks remained in the boats. But the tackle boxes, fishing rods, bait buckets and oars routinely came to the cabins. Most vacationers carried an empty coffee can and a sponge with them to bail the boat and clean it up at the end of each day. At nightfall, the dock was ready for inspection with each boat in its numbered slip ready for the next day's adventure.

When it rained there was a good possibility that we would not go fishing. When we were rained out there would be a Rummy game in the cabin. If only four played, it was Canasta. Be that as it may, Diana, my younger sister, played hostess. Midway through the game she would call a halt to the card playing and serve her version of champagne and caviar. For reasons unknown to us the cabin we usually occupied came supplied with sherbet stemware. Diana would fill the sherbet glasses with 7-Up and serve grape jelly on saltines as reasonable substitutes. We nibbled and sipped the time away waiting for someone to win the Rummy game. When we weren't playing cards, we tried our hand at jigsaw puzzles.

But sometimes it didn't rain and those were the times Dad would be fishing. He didn't always take us kids with him. For a time I was old enough to catch bait, but too young to catch fish. I was allowed to wade out into the lake with one end of the seine net and close the circle to trap a net full of minnows or I could wade offshore with a flashlight and jacklight a frog before scooping him up for the bait box. I was allowed to be bitten by mosquitoes and feasted on by leeches, but I didn't become a fishing buddy until I was older.

It was during this in-between period when I was in my early teenaged years that we discovered the Leakin' Lena.
Asher and Jesse had a son, Dwayne, who was in his early twenties. The Leakin' Lena was an old wooden flat-bottomed rowboat that Dwayne had acquired when he was a teenager. He and his friends had modified it for sailing. They had drilled a hole in the center seat and reinforced the bottom of the hull to accept a mast. They added a tiller, pulleys, and cleats. It had the basic features of a sailboat except for a keel board. With a flat bottom and no keel board, the Lena was very likely to capsize in any kind of strong wind. By the time Bobby, Diana, and I found the Lena, she was dragged up on the margin of the woods around the corner from the dock. We rolled her over and inspected her. She was ten or twelve feet long, made of wood, and once painted green. She was heavy, but this would not be a problem once we got her back in the

water. She had a front, middle and rear seat. There was room for three. Being experienced along these lines, Bobby and I went off to get Asher's approval before we moved the Lena. Asher gave his permission with the proviso that if we got her to float she had to remain behind the swimming rope.

Lake Gladstone was a depression formed when a glacier scooped it out thousands of years ago. It had a gradual slope to its bottom. One could wade out 75 yards and still be only chest deep. A swimming platform was anchored about 100 yards offshore. The platform was mainly a place to sunbathe. We were under orders not to go out to the platform without one or more of the older kids present. The swimming rope was attached to the platform and floated on white plastic buoys to mark the limits of safe water. This would be the world the Lena might explore if she would float.

We dragged her down to the water's edge. Asher had come along to supervise this operation, but when he saw us struggling to move the Lena, he lent a hand. To our surprise she floated; to no one's surprise she leaked. Therefore, she was christened the Leakin' Lena. We pushed her out into the shallow water and began to wash her out. Asher said he had something at the work shed that we might need and left us. When he got back we had washed the first layer of grime from her hull and had bailed and sponged her out. Asher had two weather-faded oars, an anchor, and a piece of rope. Asher made his own anchors. He would take empty gallon paint cans and fill them with concrete. Then he would insert a long eyebolt, with several washers and nuts threaded on it, into the concrete. When the concrete sat up, the eyebolt was secure and the rope could be attached. The cost of one of Asher's anchors was practically nothing compared to the price of a new anchor from a marine retailer. Asher tied one end of the rope to the Lena and the other to the anchor. Then he showed us how to snug the line up to keep the Lena from dragging the anchor. We were becoming "old salts".

We got screwdrivers from the work shed and tightened every screw that would still tighten. We gave her a final going over, rubbing the rust to a high sheen, before we set out on our maiden voyage. While one of us rowed, two of us bailed. This seemed to be about right to keep up with the leaks. Of course, we were forward rowers in those days. Pushing the boat along with the strength of our arms so that we could see where we were going. Later, we learned to row backwards so that the strength of our legs and backs could come into play. In the meantime, we didn't go very far or very fast. One of our oars had lost half of its blade in some long-forgotten misadventure. We discovered that rowing with a mismatched pair of oars caused us to go in circles. This was convenient in as much as we were restricted to the swimming area, but it got monotonous, so we took turns rowing and bailing. We said things like, "Yar, avast, dead ahead, aye-aye, and matey".

Asher came down to the beach carrying a green board. We asked, "What is it?" Turns out it was the tiller used during the Lena's life as a sailboat. It had been cleverly crafted using two gate pins for the pivot point. The eyes were still mounted on the stern. Asher suggested that we hang the tiller and try steering from the stern. With this arrangement we could push or pull the oars while the matey in the stern could look forward and steer to compensate for our circular rowing. But this meant that we lost one of our fulltime bailers, so our feet were often wet.

It is said that the two happiest days in a boat owner's life are the day he buys and the day he sells his boat. We were riding the wave of joy connected to new boat ownership. We had a boat just like each cabin had a boat, but our boat had once been a proud sailing vessel – "Aye, and a yar little lady she was!"

Bobby asked, "Why do you keep calling the boat a 'she'?" Remembering an old "Little Rascals" segment, which addressed the same issue, I replied, "Things of beauty, grace, and speed are usually referred to in the feminine gender." Bobby looked at me in open-mouthed wonder and said, "I guess it's because 'she's got a girl's name'".

I let it go.

Diana got a bottle of 7-Up and four sherbet glasses. We had a launching ceremony. Asher said a few words; most notably that, "no", we could not break the bottle over the bow.

We used the Lena as our swimming platform while the older kids sunbathed, showed off, and flirted on theirs. We donned our masks and fins and dove for treasure. We were Lloyd Bridges in "Sea Hunt". We were searching for the "Creature from the Black Lagoon". We were Gilbert Roland, Alan Ladd, John Wayne or any one who had ever captured our imaginations with sea adventures at a Saturday matinee. We never left the swimming area, but in our minds we had portaged to the Mississippi and were following the footsteps of La Salle and Pere Marquette.

Each night we took care of our craft. We hauled it up on the beach. We were afraid if we left it at the dock we would find it settled to the bottom by morning. So, we beached it and dutifully carried our oars to the cabin for the night. After all, we were responsible for our boat and gear.

When we came back the next summer, the Lena was gone. She had filled a gap between our childhood and adolescence. I guess we were ready to move on, but she was "yar" in her day.

…LLL

Daisies Are Fine Company

Daisies bring
   things
into a room--
   perfume
and brightness
   and lightness.

A peony
   can be lonely,
but daisies
   are always
profuse.
   Their colors
prefer
   confusion
to seclusion.

                                          ...SSG

Taps Plus One

The sun came up this morning.
You may not have noticed.
Breakfast was finished.
You may not remember.
Your clothes seem to match.
You wonder who picked them out.
Weather doesn't bother you.
You are not going out.
You feel neither hot nor cold.
You feel numb.
Numb and betrayed.
Giving into the betrayed feeling
Can only lead to anger.
Life was good.
You were on track.
But life took your friend, your lover, your husband.
A chapter ended.
Abruptly
Finally
Today should have stayed
(a little longer)
You were betrayed.
Anger will come.
NO!
Put out the "No Deliveries" sign.
Numb is safe.
Numb is comfortable.
Tonight the stars will come out.
You may not notice.

...LLL

FLYING POTATOES / STEPHEN HAWKING LIES

Recently Sir Stephen Hawking in an interview warned that the first experience of contact with another life form might end badly for humans. Professor Hawking used the image of the experience of the Natives-Americans with the American Westward movement. He in traditional English fashion did not mention the encounters between African natives and the whole of Europe, the Chinese and the Opium wars, the British Raj in India or the whole history of Africa and South America with Europe. So I have written this brief response.

This is a little heads up to those creatures
Homo sapiens - humans - people
On that orb identified as Earth
Terra Firma and Gaia
You are not alone
We are here
Too!

Now you were expecting some streamlined
Sleek saucer-shaped high-tech Frisbee
With ten-thousand running lights
Glistening in silver or white
Blasting through the
Vast void of space
Sorry to
Disappoint
See we regard
All those running lights
And pristine glowing shapes
As what you would call targets

We much prefer to burrow
Into space rubble
Floating rocks
Gnarly asteroids
Large lazy grazing cows
Discrete and comfortable
Something sensible as oxfords

No extensive streamlined design
What you might call flying potatoes
Just a thick mantle of igneous insulate
In floating fields of similar
Bumper car potatoes
Bit of gravitational spin
Hundred recessed eyes
With which to view
The passing parade
Of fat slow planets
Sending out beams
Of senseless babble
Revealing their location
Weakness wealth and inability
To organize a coherent command structure for defense

Ignore Stephen Hawking's paranoid blather
We come in peace we are your friends
We have your best interest at heart
We never intend you any harm
So long as the grass is green
And the sky is blue.

            …JBM

Song to Myself

Pity the butterfly who
struggles through a series
of fat caterpillar skins
to become a wet lump
hung from a bough menaced
by even its friend, the wind.
Then emerging fragile,
inadequate, it trembles
on the branch--again in peril--
until its only recourse
is to learn to soar.

...SSG

The Autopsy

The eyes
bright shining stars no longer
now stare
in shock and awe
from cheeks
my hand would cup
to wipe
a trail of crusted tears.

No sweet juices
pass thirstily thru these lips
glistening
their small white teeth
into a smile,
just bitter tastes of death
choked
a boy's slender throat.

The lungs
under this smooth chest
once pink
and pumping air
turned grey
breathing black ash
of hatred
from our fetid smoke.

The heart
that raced down
barefoot streets
in the ignorance
of joy
pounded future rhythms
and stopped
when the last wall broke.

The mind
and all the things it will
never know
cowered in corners
covered
by a mother
whose voice
was his last small hope.

The soul
is sliced precisely
from its womb
by a scalpel
seeking answers.
The operation
is over.
Another war is won.

        ...SSG

Little Poems Six

12/17/1903 Orville Wright made the first controlled, powered flight (12 seconds, 120 feet) at Kitty Hawk in North Carolina in the Wright Flyer.

    Wilbur and Orville Wright
    Two men on a one-man flight
    This fact should not be overlooked
    Man's first flight was overbooked

7/17/1938 Douglas Corrigan earned the name "Wrong Way" by leaving New York on a flight plan for California and 29 hours later arriving in Ireland.

    Douglas "Wrong Way" Corrigan
    Won't make that mistake again
    His flight plan said ◀, he went ▶
    He might still be ▲, if he hadn't come ▼.

    …LLL

TO A TEXAS POTHOLE

GOD blessed the potholes of Texas
They have been fruitful and multiplied
And everything is bigger in Texas

Something shiny in a Texas pothole
It's either oil, blood
Or a four-wheel drive

Why do you think we wear cowboy boots?
There hasn't been a cattle drive
In a hundred years

It's why they invented
The Texas two-step

...JBM

Barren Tree

Winter's killing hand
delights the barren trees
now all are alike

...SSG

Cranes

Cranes legs grow longer
as rocks appear in our pond--
Summer drought wins out

...SSG

CELIBATE

I awoke this morning in a good mood

Redeemed only by that mantra

Of this too will pass

I looked into the mirror amazed

That I have yet again grown in girth

And one day uglier

And I thought to myself

Surely there must be children somewhere

I could frighten into lives

As celibate monks.

                                            ...JBM

Love is Relative

Tomorrow's love is
    a many-splendored thing.

Today's love is
    a molly-coddled clinging.

Yesterday's love is
    a moldy codfish.

                                                ...SSG

Divine Circumspection

I have confined my mind
to this porch whose windows
look out on time
one tree
two bushes
garden of my design
a fence that's high
and made of wood.

My cats are walkabouts.
I fear their forays out.
They crawl beneath the fence
and clamber high in trees.
These emissaries
from foreign streets
bring tiny dead things back
as proof that life exists.

And thus my yard is littered
with carcasses
like everyone's--
but they belong in mine.
All sacred things should be
in places this sublime,
where every blade of grass
measures holy time.

…SSG

HODAR* SALUTE

(To the tune of Clementine.)

You're our DARlings,
You're our DARlings
You're our D-A-R-lings, one and all.
Daughters of the Revolution,
Born of rebels with a cause.

You're our DARlings,
You're our DARlings,
You're our D-A-R-lings, one and all.
A grateful nation's unsung legion,
Answering still the patriots' call.

You're our DARlings,
You're our DARlings,
You're our D-A-R-lings, one and all.
Sisters bound in common purpose,
You are DARlings, one and all.

...LLL

*Husband of the Daughters of the American Revolution

SCHMALTZ

Butterflies can't sing
Even in the Japanese
Painted on their wings
Ideograms
T'ai Chi dance
But carry a tune
Not a chance

Don't let them fool you
When they come
Knocking on the door
Selling cookies, candy bars
And raffle tickets

Butterflies can't sing
They just flap their wings
Sometimes beauty is silent
Chased by children through
The endless gardens
And creating Tsunami
Across the globe

...JBM

Benny

Benny was one of those individuals who happened upon a magic lantern and freed a genie by mistake. Naturally the genie offered him a three-wish reward, which Benny accepted. When he had made his wishes, the genie informed him that there was a condition: Benny was not to shave, cut his hair, or in any other way remove it for the rest of his life. Benny quickly agreed. The genie cautioned him, "The minute you cut your hair I will turn you in to a pot, like a big, old Greek wine pot." For a while Benny was happy with all the money, women and power he could wish for, but eventually his hair got to him. It was long and nasty. It tripped him. It stank. It was greasy. So, Benny got himself a shave, a haircut, and a bikini-wax job. He was immediately transformed into a Grecian urn, because a Benny shaved is a Benny urned.

...LLL

Chapter Seven

Uncle Coot	JBM
Parapraxis	SSG
Little Poems Seven	LLL
Let the Party	JBM
Exercise in Youth	SSG
Widows Walk	SSG
Silhouette	JBM
Father's History	SSG
Pledge Sunday	LLL
Trickledown Survivor	JBM
The Cat-astrophes	SSG
Close Call	SSG
The Burdens of Youth	JBM
Disco	LLL

UNCLE "COOT"

Writers do not have flaws, but rather facets of character. Like my Uncle "Coot" Matson who had about a two quart a day facet to him. If he had any other facets or redeeming qualities, I passed out long before they emerged.

Now "Old Coot" as everyone called him, among other things, believed in a non-materialist lifestyle and so lived in the back of a pickup truck. Not a camper, mind you, but the back of a pickup truck, and he didn't own so much as an outdoor privy. Excuse me ladies, but there was dogs that wouldn't walk on the downwind side of that man. Hell, they even say he voted Republican once, but I think it bad manners to speak ill of the dead.

He never missed a church supper, ice cream social, pot luck dinner, wedding reception, or an after funeral spread even though he was not what you would call on the guest list.

He was a writer locally known but not widely read. Mostly letters to the Editor, several Congressmen, a few Senators, and all the Supreme Court Judges and of course every President. We all knew about these letters mostly because they were never delivered. You see Uncle "Coot" refused to put postage stamps on them as they were in his own words, "Official business between a Congressman and his constituent," and if every huckster in saddle oxfords and a Seersucker suit could deduct the cost of air fare and hotel when they went to meet their Congressman in a dark parking lot he felt the post office could, "deliver his insight and advice gratis". Franking privilege, he called it, though I assure you it was a little rawer than frank. Needless to say the local Postmaster did not share "Coot's" view.

That was why "Coot" voted in every election, showed up for every Council meeting, attended every political rally and every civic function from the fire station openings to the parking meter installation on Main Street for thirty-eight years, though he claimed it was longer.

"Old Coot" died quietly during a Baptist revival at the age of ninety-four shortly before the altar call which he would usually answer as it had been several months since he was last saved. He always tried to get saved at least four times a year unless it was an election year as an example to the other suckers for the tearful very specific confession.

One of the Ministers at his funeral (they drew straws) said he might be in heaven what with his having been saved regularly, but doubted he would go someplace where he didn't know anybody.

...JBM

Parapraxis

By 1909 Carl Jung was considered Sigmund Freud's heir apparent. That year, during a boat trip to America, Jung told Freud of a dream he had about him. Freud fainted, as he perceived the dream to reflect Jung's death wish for him.

My superego is dying
and not with dignity.
Even now it dances wildly
round the fire of id--
like a shaman who chants
to keep himself in power
and hold the truth at bay.
Eventually I'm sure the ego
will perceive some weakness
in the magic chains that slipped
around his hands and feet
when he was young
and apparently asleep.
The ego senses breakdown
like a warrior senses blood.
Once the seep begins
it's impossible to hold.
When the superego fails
the fire will self-implode.

...SSG

Little Poems Seven

Abraham Lincoln did you say?
I think I heerd ah him back a way.
My memory may have slipped some cogs.
Did he invent those Lincoln Logs?

Truman Capote
Had <u>Breakfast At Tiffany's.</u>
His popularity ebbed its flood
When he finished <u>In Cold Blood</u>.

Snoopy watched the sun make the snowman droopy.
Then to his eyes the tears arose.
Still, he was not too upset
To eat the snowman's carrot nose.

George Eliot
Her <u>Silas Marner</u> did sell a lot
Accepted her fame magnanimously
Of course, she published anonymously.

>   …LLL

LET THE PARTY

When there's a brief lull in the party
When the band takes a break
Let me slip through some side door
Into the cool dark of an endless night
To lay in the grass on my back
And watch the stars glide past

I want to leave before the party is over,
Before the band comes back
I want to breathe out before
The last notes of dance
I want to hear the tinkling laughter
And party murmurs fade

Into the endless ratchet of crickets
And the susurration through the leaves

I do not wish
To be missed
Let the party
go on

Without me.

...JBM

Exercise in Youth

    We were thin when we were young.
The boys smiled. We were not afraid.
    Those six flights up seemed like fun.

    Our bodies stayed in the sun,
and risked no death by getting laid.
    We were thin when we were young.

    "Reefer Madness" was all we'd done,
most other laws we had obeyed.
    Those six flights up seemed like fun.

    Our dance with life had just begun.
We didn't even pull the shade.
    We were thin when we were young.

    We weren't afraid to eat the bun.
Our skin had not begun to fade.
    Those six flights up seemed like fun.

    Now I puff when I start to run.
I can't remember when I've weighed.
    We were thin when we were young.
Those six flights up seemed like fun.

    …SSG

The Widows Walk

I watch the widows walk

beneath my window.

Leaves have fallen round them.

Clasping arms they weave

their way through dead wood

on petrified legs.

Clutching shrunken wombs

they are gray with words.

I wonder at

the numbness of my toes

...SSG

SILHOUETTE

Epigraph: In memory of Jake Byrd (06/07/1998) 49 years old; Jake Robel (02/22/2000) 6 years old.

What was it like in those first few seconds?
When the chain gripped the ankles
The tarmacadam ripped the flesh
Clothes torn away the big man fought for life
Tried to raise his head
Three miles in chains
On Huff Creek Road, Jasper Texas
One June day in 1998
Head, arm, and torso three miles apart
And that boy, just six, held in a safety belt
Five miles along the Interstate
Images your mind creates
As a boy I saw a man dragged by a railroad car
Down a cinder strewn alley, a flailing rag doll
Caught in the axel, stripped of his flesh
Screaming to his brother to pull the brake
Images you don't forget
Decades later I saw my first mass burn victim
A woman in her seventies, chemical coma
Her two sisters' victims of an electric heater
Her lips and flesh just beginning to swell
And weep the fluids of life away
Even years later I imagine the scene
Three elderly women one with nightgown on fire
The two sisters who tried to beat the flames out
Till all three were burning

Images your mind creates
The doctor's orders were simple
As much pain medication as she needs
She was gone the next day
Before my shift started
I knew her name once
Images you don't forget.

Postscript: The iron fence no longer separates the graves of whites and blacks in the 171-year-old cemetery where James Byrd is buried.)

...JBM

Father's History

    From the back of the car
your words are softened by age
    and can barely be heard.
They are lost in the sound
    of the road and the wind.

    We gaze out our window
intent on pretending we know
    how this road used to go;
where there once was a bridge:
    and whose fields were found here.

    But the details are lost
in the roar of our rush
    as we try to outrun
the endlessly chirping crickets
    who warn that evening is come.

    So the sounds of your past
mix with the drone of the tires
    and the hum of the engine
until at last I can hear
    your steadily beating heart.

                                                …SSG

Pledge Sunday

Bear with me a minute as I describe some needs of the church.
Then you decide what the Lord is leading you to do.

At any given moment the church may need:

Bulletin inserts and paper clips,
Youth group leaders and potato chips,
Carpet cleaning and new roof tiles,
Sunday greeters with friendly smiles,
Parking lot stripes and asphalt sealers,
Doorbell dinners and cheerful healers,
Choir directors and robe dry cleaning,
Pithy sermons all filled with meaning,
Desktop publishing and copier toners,
Volunteer schedules and telephoners,
Hand bell ringers and solo singers,
Cookie walkers and cookie bringers,
Bibles and hymnals and pulpit supply,
Hand soap and tissue – always two ply,
Piano tuners and an audio system,
Postage stamps and hands to stick 'em,
Office staff and custodians too,
Mid-week series and Wednesday night stew,
VCS and VCR
DVD and a strummed guitar,
A quiet place for babies and dads,
Pencils, candles and friendship pads,
Chancel flowers and palms for parading,
Salaries and pensions that need upgrading,

G. A., Synod and Presbytery,
Parish Associate and Missionary,
Compassion child and Day Care dollars,
Wee Kirk fund and Preschool scholars,
These things are needed and so are you.
Only you can decide what you will do.
On November 18, and this is not hard,
Bring your Operating Budget Commitment card.
If the green card mailing failed to reach ya,
Drop by the office and tell the preacher.

Amen

...LLL

TRICKLEDOWN SURVIVOR

I saw a young man today
Pushing a shopping cart
Loaded with trash bags
Presumably
All his worldly possessions
And I wondered if anyone
Had spoken to him
About rampant materialism
Recently
Conversely I wondered
How many
...I said not now
...Don't you sass me boy
...Back of the hands
It had taken to launch
This fragile jury-rig youth
Upon the sea of life
Nah it was probably
His own damned fault
Ran with the wrong crowd
Played that music too damned loud
Booze and a bad Momma
Never appreciated anything
Or did a lick of work
In his entire life
Of twenty years
But then
Perhaps there had been
Too many cliché's
Never enough praise
There never seem to be
Enough "attaboys" to go around
There's a long cold winter coming on
And there's a boy pushing
A shopping cart down the street
Somebody ought to do something
Maybe they should bring back the draft

...JBM

The Cat-astrophes

A cataclysm has occurred.
Victims race, frantic
to escape death.
Yowls of pain echo
the path of injury.
Along the way
tufts of hair,
traces of blood,
These tiny bits,
could they be bone?
Remnants of a war
as shrieks implied?

A colossus stands
astride the carnage
weapon at her side.
Survivors cower in corners.
Their claws too
will soon be trimmed,
and death is sure to follow.

...SSG

Close Call

It's too early to hear the owl
that speaks to shadows.
I thank the winter wren
whose sudden song cuts through
like sunlight across my floor.

But she leaves behind more starkness--
a larger hole than before.
Foliage flutters from unknown breath.
Small eyes blink unseen.
Silence waits for time to end.

Until one dog barks no.

...SSG

THE BURDENS OF YOUTH

It is hard being young
There is almost nothing you can do
Every single person on the planet
Already knows how to fly an airplane
Drive a car, skateboard or ride a bicycle
But you are too young, too little,
Too short, too small
Or your legs are not long enough
Everyone tells you you're cute
But no one asks you out on a date
Ten year olds tell you
You are gross
They don't want to be your playmate
This is just for big kids
You can't keep up, you'll just get hurt
Imagine living in a world where everyone
Knows how to tie their shoes – except you
The universe has plotted against you
Why you can't even put on a tee-shirt
That isn't backwards, wrong side
With the label sticking out
And this indignity from a tee-shirt
Buttons and holes never match
Shoes go on the wrong foot just fine
But some Adult will spot it every time
And there you stand
One black, one brown
"Consider the lilies of the field
Was Solomon in all his glory
Arrayed as one of these?"
No and you better not pick
Any of the neighbor's flowers.

...JBM

Disco

Sam, "the Clam," ran a nightclub in California. Sam never said much, but he had the hottest dance music and the coldest beer around. When disco dancing was popular, musicians from all over the area (and farther away) came to hear what was new. An off-duty angel fluttered by one night and heard the band. She thought to herself, "I don't have the duty until tomorrow afternoon; I think I'll go down there." – So she did. The band made a place for her and her harp. They played heavenly music and drank cold beer until the wee hours of the morning. She awoke in Heaven the next day a little groggy and barely made it to angel formation. When her superior angel asked her, "Where is your instrument?" She said, "Oh no! I left my harp in Sam Clam's disco."

...LLL

Chapter Eight

Cherchez La Femme	LLL
Japanese Tea Garden	SSG
I Think	LLL
Genius	JBM
The Lost Soles	SSG
Our Crisis	SSG
Fallen Trees	JBM
Psycho Chefs & Paranoid Potatoes	JBM
I Grow Old	SSG
Neighbor's Chimes	SSG
November	LLL
The Devil You Say	JBM
In Tune	SSG
Little Poems Eight	LLL
Sister Deloris	JBM
US Mail	LLL

CHERCHEZ LA FEMME

During the war years and the late forties, Mom was preoccupied with having and raising children. Still, she also made time to open and operate a delicatessen in St. Louis. We lived in the back of the store. Mom was her own boss. Oh, she helped a friend with a catering service from time to time and after we moved to the county she worked the candy counter at the Woolworth's store. But in 1954 she took her first *status* job. She became the receptionist for the local Dodge-Chrysler dealership. Her duties included answering the telephone, taking messages, fixing snack trays, greeting customers and offering beverages. With children ages 10, 11 and 15, there was a good deal of overlap in her job descriptions.

She was enthusiastic about her role as the receptionist; she was a flight attendant without an airplane. She liked the sound of the word – receptionist. She took pride in it. She wanted to be identified with her work. She was happy. She saw herself as being on the cutting edge of the women's movement. She was an independent woman, yet vital and loyal to the dealership. It embarrassed her that her husband drove a Mercury.

In the winter of 1954-1955 Dodge came out with a new product – the *La Femme. The* Chrysler Corporation® determined that the time was ripe to introduce a vehicle designed specifically for the modern American woman. To accomplish this end, a fashion designer was hired to coordinate accessories. The car, itself, was a Dodge Custom Royal Lancer equipped with a V-8 engine, PowerFlite™ fully automatic transmission, power brakes and power steering. In short this was a heavy piece of machinery with enough amenities that even a small woman could handle it easily in traffic.

The accessorizing of the *La Femme* took the concept of a woman's car from the drawing board to the marketplace. The color scheme and interior were breathtaking. The *La Femme* had a two-toned color scheme of Heather Rose over Sapphire White. The Heather Rose was the shade of pale pink strawberry ice cream. The Sapphire White looked creamy like evaporated milk. The normal chrome lettering was replaced by yellow metal suggesting gold. The silver *Custom Royal Lancer* on the front fender was replaced with the gold *La Femme*. The interior was appointed with pink-flecked white carpeting, pink vinyl and rose-patterned pink tapestry. The backside of the driver and passenger seats held a surprise. There were pink leather compartments. The driver's side compartment held a pink rose-patterned raincoat, rain hat and umbrella. There was room for maps as well. But the passenger seat compartment held the *coup de grace*: There was a pink calfskin purse made to fit like a keystone into the compartment, and the purse was accessorized. In the purse were a lipstick case, a compact, a change purse, a cigarette case, and a cigarette lighter —all in rose pink leather and gold-look metal.

Naturally, my mother fell in love with the car when she heard of its existence. She could not wait for its appearance on the show-room floor. She was as nervous as teen-aged girls waiting for Eddie Fisher to come on stage. When it arrived she had trouble serving coffee and greeting customers with that pink beauty sitting right there next to her telephone-answering desk. She began chipping away at my father's resistance. She convinced him that his 1949 Mercury® was too out of date for a man in a middle management position. Besides it would soon be in need of costly repairs. *We* needed a car. Shelby would be driving soon. *We* needed a car. With Shelby and Mom both driving, we needed something designed for women. *We* needed *this* car.

So Dad was worn down and we became the owners of a Dodge *La Femme*. Estimates are that there may have been as many as 2500 or as few as 500 of these cars made during the 1955-1956 production years. It was possible to live happily through the 50s without ever hearing of the *La Femme* much less seeing one. *We owned one.*

The newness of our *La Femme* had begun to fade when it was time to pack for the summer trip to Lake Gladstone. Mom was still showing her car off every time anyone commented on this original "Pink Lady". Dad did not share her enthusiasm, but he was a good sport about it. He took his turn in the car pool and endured the kidding.

When we got to Minnesota in the summer of 1955, Asher and Jessie greeted us and complimented our new car. Mom, of course, took this as a request to demonstrate its features. Don, Marian and son, Bobby, were in the resort, but held back on coming over to greet us until Mom's spiel was ended. Don and Dad greeted each other with their usual handshake and began to talk with Asher about fishing. Don did not mention the car. As the unloading proceeded, the car was forgotten.

Later that evening, we sat on the screened porch thankful to be out of the reach of the mosquitoes. Mom and Marian had gone in to fix popcorn and drinks. Don turned to Dad and began to talk about Peoria, IL.

"You know Peoria has the Caterpillar plant and related industry. We get a pretty good piece of the convention business as well. Earlier this year I met a man who was in Peoria to receive some kind of sales award. I met him the night he got his award. He seemed uncomfortable as I sat down beside him at the coffee counter. He was dressed in a soft pastel yellow suit and a matching yellow tie with a contrasting pattern of pale blue flowers. I was thinking about what this might mean when he interrupted my musings. He proclaimed himself to be an ordinary guy with a wife and family. He assured me his attire did not imply anything. He continued, 'I was away from home last week when I was notified of this award. I realized I needed a new suit. I called my wife. I asked her to go to Cox's Department store, pick out a seersucker suit: size 42 regular, 30-inch inseam, and have it delivered to my hotel. She went to Sears®…'"

Don paused, looked over his glasses at Dad and said, "So, you have a pink car."

When the 1957 models came out, Dad bit the depreciation bullet and traded the *La Femme* on a blue and white Dodge Lancer.

Mom kept the cigarette lighter.

…LLL

Japanese tea garden

the lone pink blossom
awaits
the white butterfly.

...SSG

I Think

I think
Mason Williams wrote,
"Dylan Thomas has come and gone,
Come and gone, come and gone.
Dylan Thomas has come and gone;
His blood turned to words."

Rod McKuen wrote,
"I try to be a good beatnik,
But it's hard."

The Gospel writer John wrote,
"In the beginning was the Word,
And the Word was with God
And the Word was God."

Maybe we are a Word
Returning to the Word
And
Whatever we try to be good at
In the meantime is going to be hard.

But I could be wrong.

...LLL

Genius

I hear the sound of time passing
In the night.

I wake up my mate who says:
"That's the bathroom faucet
I told you to fix it two weeks ago."

It is sad my mate's
Memory is failing so
I am sure it was last February

A year ago.

                                        ...JBM

The Lost Soles

Today it was a flip-flop
yesterday a laced up shoe,
tomorrow a dirty sneaker
with tongue hanging out.
Each has seen enough
and sits silently in the road,
suddenly unnecessary.
Snatched from the foot
of some raptured soul,
or lost in the struggle
when the aliens came
and left in the night.

Or maybe they just
were never wanted
by the one-legged man
who steals our socks.

...SSG

Our Crisis

The fast hand of fate

snatches the sun

leaving us stunned

standing in the shadow

of our soul.

...SSG

Fallen Trees

It's easier not to think about death
The cold clutching hand
The last gasping breath

The Universe as we know it
Making a final curtain call

I have been there many times before
Visited that distant shore

And I am here to tell you friend
There is no end in the end

The dice roll on, the roulette wheel spins
The cards are turned over and over again
And it's always another game another hand

Fear not for how else could
Eternity be an eternity

There must be an ear within the forest
To hear the tree fall

Of course we won't be there
Perhaps the tax collectors will be.

...JBM

Psycho Chefs and Paranoid Potatoes

(SILENCE OF THE YAMS)

Are potatoes paranoid?
Hiding there beneath the soil
Sending out trailing vines
Watching with a hundred eyes

Burrowing in dark root cellar
Huddling in a gunnysack
Listening for creaking steps
Misery of cold and damp

You'd think we were going
To skin them alive
Boil them in oil
Or cut out their eyes

Come on up little fellow
I've a warm bath waiting
In salted water
Maybe even a pat of butter

And a little dash of pepper!

...JBM

I Grow Old

They've come in the night
and stolen my clothes.
The christening dress
with embroidered rose,
the overalls worn to play,
the pleated skirt for school,
the bra undone by you.

With all high heels, low heels
and padded suits they've fled.

Now I'm left with a naked soul
in a roomful of people I don't know.

…SSG

Neighbors Chimes

Neighbors tinkling chimes
disrupt my summer slumber--
too many new wings.

...SSG

NOVEMBER

November cold—when winter first gets its foot in the door
and the rain comes
making the days gray.
November cold—the first forecast of winter.
Harbinger of winter.
With that first nip in October
the wardrobe yielded its long sleeves
and wool sweaters.
Now the first cold of winter is hinted at
in the November sky.
The days are gray and rain has come back
to break the sere of summer.
The sky is heavy.
The clouds bend to earth
slapping the leaves off the trees.
And so we rake leaves.

A few weeks ago the leaves were dry
under the rake
and they rustled like petticoats
at a square dance.
The air was clear
and the sunshine made the work annoying.
This was the kind of day meant for play
to roll in the leaf piles and laugh.

The leaves crunch under the rake.
Have you ever seen such a rake?
Metal tines with a spring-loaded backbone
bought thirty-five years ago
when burning was allowed.

A man needed a metal rake then
to contain the fire in a neat circle
or to catch the wayward cluster
of glowing leaf embers
rising on the air currents
coming from the bowels
of the burning barrel.
This is a solid rake
the kind to last a lifetime
and it has, and it has.

There was smoke then,
the autumn afternoon was punctuated by
the smell of leaves burning
and fireplaces being tested against
the coming winter nights
when crackling fires, marshmallows and hot chocolate
would take the place of leaf smoke.

Today the metal rake goes unused.
The rake has gone the way of
fielders' mitts and tennis rackets
oversized,
oversized and made of plastic.
The sound of wet November leaves
against plastic tines
is more a moan than a song
Skarooch…Skarooch…Skarooch…

Wet November.

…LLL

THE DEVIL YOU SAY

Poor old Satan father of lies
Nary given word of credit
For protecting the family name
Keeping all of those shameful secrets
How he got that chocolate cake
Named for him I'll never know
No one ever says a kind word about him

Say what you will
He was good to his Momma
He grew the most beautiful roses
Made the best corn liquor
Always voted Republican
So far as I know

They do not build Cathedrals in his honor
Or endow scholarships in his name
But one thing you got to say for sure
No matter how many mistakes you made in life
He never turned anybody away from his door

…JBM

In Tune

Moonlight sonata
I
don't think we oughta-
go.

...SSG

Little Poems Eight

Thought Lot,
A guy should be happy with what he's got.
That his wife looked back was not his fault…
Besides, a guy can always use a little salt.

In 1786, John Fitch
Built the first working steamboat and thought he'd be rich,
But his dreams were sunk and he lived to regret it
Robert Fulton got the patents, the cash, and the credit.

Said Emeril Lagassi, a chef with flair,
When he catered a mathematicians' affair,
"Diced beets, potatoes, and carrots in soups –
These number crunchers really love their cubed roots."

Mathematician Karl F. Gauss
From frequency studies made around the house
Plotted the curve of the normal distribution
And started a grading revolution.

>   …LLL

SISTER DELORIS

Sister Deloris black cowl and the Iron Cross
Swept through the lunch room doors
With the silent assurance of a battlefield commander
Surveying the scythe, swing, thrust and parry
Of armored tanks at El al Amine in Rommel's dessert
Where Montgomery and Patton made their fame
Long before the soft Sicilian underbelly
She could smell trouble like cordite
And burning oil slicks amid the Saharan heat

A phalanx of sixth graders
Froze silent in their seats
Turned to their plates and pretended to eat
As a barrage of chatter in the third grade corner
Turned to bowed heads and pale trembling lipped faces
Every waxed paper sandwich was opened with the care
Of an Engineer Corp clearing a mine field
One soft slow blade thrust at a time
In a series of radar sweeps
Her eyes locked onto
The wolves and sheep

There was little fat Patty
Brought to tears by unending petty taunts and jeers
Till Sister Deloris
Found her singing voice
And sealed her promotion into the fifth grade royalty

There was the pug nosed Thompson boy
Didn't have a friend in the world
Fight at the drop of a stick of chalk
Until he had that ten minute talk
With Sister Deloris
Prayer Card and an artist sketch pad
Turns out he could draw dogs, horses
And spell like a champ

And Eddie Monaco
With thick coke bottle glasses
His standing secured with a little elastic
To hold those glasses in their place
Now regularly anointed that special grace
Relief pitcher and first base

Her ears honed in on an unsavory mirth
Of giggles and tears as she moved across the room
For the little tables with their back turned
Where the fourth graders sat

She was in their midst with her fingers pointed
Crushing that small ring of laughter
Around one tearful boy pink-faced with frustration's rage
At the sight of his lunch sandwich paper folded back
Revealing a sandwich of Peanut butter and Brussels sprouts

A Peanut butter and Brussels sprouts sandwich
Sister Deloris caught her breath
What level of poverty
What kind of a parent
In her mind flashed
Would feed a child
On such as this?

Then her anger fury and fire was caught in mid heart-beat
As a gap toothed boy his face tear streaked
Looked up at her his small dignity shattered
And said, "Momma knows
I don't like wheat bread."

…JBM

US Mail

In the early years of this nation, mail was not so much delivered as it was picked up. The postmaster or postmistress designated a location in the community where one could receive mail. It was not until after the Civil War that the federal government began to hire men to deliver mail directly to private homes in the larger cities. This system of patronage was expanded after the Spanish-American War and the Great War (WW I) to provide jobs for returning veterans. The automobile in the 1920s helped expand mail delivery into the farmlands. Mail carriers were issued posthole diggers, augers and tamping rods to assist homeowners in setting rural mailboxes to meet regulations. It was not unusual for the postmaster to allow the carriers to use these tools during their off hours. Many a carrier earned extra money in their spare time by helping farmers set fence posts. It was this period of our nation's history that first saw the widespread use of the term U.S. Post Hole Service.

...LLL

Chapter Nine

Seashells	LLL
A Modest Fantasy	SSG
Chance Encounter	JBM
The Man Who Measured Time	SSG
Gravy in a Jar	JBM
The World Spins Its Bottle	SSG
Orinoco	JBM
Pieces	SSG
Little Poems Nine	LLL
The Fallen	JBM
Period	SSG
Facing Rejection	JBM
Prayer Takes Many Forms	LLL
Pliny's Curse	JBM
Teeth	LLL

Seashells

She seemed uncertain. She stood on the beach bent slightly forward holding a seashell. She seemed undecided. Would she stand up? Or, would she bend down and return the seashell to the sand? She hesitated. She glanced toward her companion and a sort of a moan came from deep in her chest, "I don't understand..."

Randy and I were partners before our retirements. Over the years we learned to read each other and sense what the other was about to do or say. It was as if we had a pre-wireless wireless connection. He might begin to sing a lyric from the middle of an 'oldie' only to have me finish the verse. A co-worker might ask a question and we would both respond like a pair of tag team wrestlers. One might say we had psychic rapport.

We came to the beach with our wives. As they walked down the beach, we stopped for a while. He talked about the restoration he was doing on an MG-A series sports car. I clicked on the camera feature of my phone to get a picture of a pelican. Neither of us paid any attention to the two women approaching us.

One of them stopped within a few yards of us and bent to dig a seashell from the sand.

"I've had my eye on that one," Randy said loudly.

She sensed he was speaking to her. She looked at him.

He repeated, "I've had my eye on that shell. I thought it looked good where it was."

Taking my cue from Randy I stepped up and gestured toward him, "You may not be aware, this man owns what is possibly the world's largest collection of seashells. He keeps them spread out on beaches around the globe for the public to enjoy. You are not supposed to disturb the displays." I waited for my words to sink in.

The tourist chewed on the explanation for a while and the moan began to well up until it burst forth, "I don't understand."

Only then did we hear her northern European accent and realize our joke had fallen on foreign ears.

Randy magnanimously said, "It's alright. You may have that seashell." He paused before encouraging her to, "Go ahead; take it."

With those parting words, we turned away and they walked away.

We didn't try to explain.

Somewhere in northern Europe a woman (perhaps two) may still believe there is a mad man in Florida who thinks he owns the world's seashells.

Somewhere in Florida a responsible senior citizen (perhaps two) is preparing another act of craziness.

A person can only have a finite number of pelican pictures.

…LLL

A Modest Fantasy

The incessant beeping
of a truck backing--
how far can it go?
Over a cliff I hope,
bouncing loudly against the rocks
and smashing to bits in the end.
It's down there now with all
the screeching car alarms,
the booming bass, the filthy rap,
the unmuffled of the world.
They are filling the canyon now.
I'd bulldoze them over
in my dreams, but the bulldozers
are down there too.

...SSG

CHANCE ENCOUNTER

I think I met an angel today
In fact I am quite sure I did
Disguised of course
No wings, harps, haloes,
Or floating white gowns
Not even a puffy little cloud
But an angel nonetheless
In disguise as I said

Angels do come and go
In disguises you know
They do not have to appear whole
But hidden in the aroma
Of baking bread, cinnamon buns
The colors of flowers
Even in a child's smile

But my angel came disguised
As a book
Now who would have thought?
Such things do not happen
But Balaam himself
Spoke with an ass
I have spoken to a few myself
And they weren't even angels

A book you see
Is a great hiding place
You have heard
The question asked
How many angels can dance
On the head of a pin?

Imagine how many
On the dots in a book.

...JBM

The Man Who Measured Time

The man in spandex
began my day
from t-shirt to sweatshirt
from no cap to ball cap
to ear muffs and gloves
his wardrobe measured
the inching up of time.

Our larger leaps
were measured by the foot
the long-stride run
the short step jog
the slowed down trot
the speed walk roll.

He may have reached
a slower shuffle now.
The fact that I don't know
tells something of our lives.
I'm no longer up at dawn.
He, perhaps, ran out of time.

...SSG

Gravy in a Jar

I remember the good old days
When you could buy a nickel cup of coffee
With a little container of cream
A bag of chips and a candy bar for the same price
Not the same nickel

Bread was ten cents a loaf
And twenty-five cents worth of lunch meat
Could feed a family of eight for a week
(Perhaps I exaggerate a little)

Frozen food was ice cream
Al dente hadn't been invented
Everything was cooked well done
Nobody took E. coli for granted
And gravy did not come in a jar!

My Momma learned to make gravy in the Depression
Pan drippings fried flour and milk together
Made biscuits out of flour and water
Made dumplings out of flour and water
Made noodles out of flour and water
People ate a lot of flour and water in those days
Because it stuck to your ribs just like paste
(Which is made out of flour and water)

Now in my lifetime I have seen grown men
With workmen appetites
Pass up fried chicken and bone-in pork chops
To eat my Momma's gravy
Even on store-bought white bread
I've seen these same men on a first visit
Lift breakfast plates of gravy and biscuits
To stumble teary-eyed to the kitchen
Crying, "Momma, Momma!
Is it you Momma?"

Out in a restaurant the other night
I saw a man take the lid off of a salt shaker
So he could season his gravy right
And not fool around with them little-bitty holes
But his wife did him one better
When she got the lid off the pepper shaker
I had to admire their efforts
To get a home cooked meal
When dining out

I don't know why they stopped making gravy
I guess it went out with the fried food
Butter and sugar bowls with real sugar
You can't make gravy in a microwave
They say it's not good for you anyway
I have friends who buy gravy in a jar
They are Republicans mostly
But I don't trust gravy in a jar
It's un-American.

                                ...JBM

The world spins its bottle

The world spins its bottle
and kisses where it lands.
Birth collides a thousand things
I choose to worship or malign.
    (Voodoo kings yank my strings)

The world spins its bottle
and kisses where it lands.
I connect the stars like dots
to form the gods of my design.
    (Voodoo kings yank my strings)

The world spins its bottle
and kisses where it lands.
Physicists use phantom fingers
to draw imaginary lines.
    (Voodoo kings yank my strings)

The world spins its bottle
and kisses where it lands.
Economists use invisible hands
to thumb their scales.
    (Voodoo kings yank my strings)

The world spins its bottle
and kisses where it lands.
Death drops like a rock in a pond,
scatters a thousand things.
    (None of them are voodoo kings)

The world spins its bottle
and kisses where it lands.
A miter reads a mind
so certain souls become divine.
    (Voodoo kings still yank my strings)

My life is permutations,
neither tabula rasa nor design.
The world spins its bottle
and kisses where it lands.
    (That's the plan).

                                                  ...SSG

ORINOCO

The day they buried Elizabeth Anetheis
The sun shone brightly, content
A few small tears of joy, heaven sent
As one of GOD'S little annoyances
Had been resolved
Even Hell celebrated
At the return of one of it's
Founding members
She had been an upright woman
Who treated everyone the same
So long as you were Christian, white
And she could pronounce your name
Regarded her peers on serious matters
Wardrobes, merchant discounts and social status
Who would now count the months?
From nuptials to natal
Comment that color of hair or eyes
Did not match forbearers
In either family line
But bore strong resemblance
To hired hand or a neighbor
Credited often with repeating gossip
Which wasn't true
She was far more likely to originate
Or so embellish that even simple solo piece
Took on symphonic airs
Imagine the Boston Pops doing
Twinkle, Twinkle Little Star
Or Old MacDonald had a Farm
Long ago she learned to look at eyebrows
Instead of the eyes

When she wanted to appear sincere
The woman could stare down a pig
She was always first to call
To express her sympathy
To whatever family
Was with new scandal plagued
For surely they would be
Humiliated embarrassed ashamed
And there were always further details
To wheedle out to expound
When you tried to buy a mobile home
The bankers turned down your loan
Nobody's business but your own
Till Elizabeth Anetheis got on the phone
Full of advice encouragement wisdom
Just sticking her nose into your business
When a spouse got drunk or a child arrested
When you visited a clinic to be tested
She would know the results before your physician
Was your car repossessed?
Did your daughter get undressed?
Who spread the story bet you guessed
Local gossips would for once be speechless
That this mighty Orinoco of innuendo
Would cease flow overnight
Was GOD thinning the herd
With an aimed curare tipped dart
Delivered on a wisp of air for the heart
Whenever the world made an unkind remark
Elizabeth Anetheis was sure to be there.

...JBM

Pieces

From atoms, particles
    and molecules
to cosmos, galaxies
    and stars.
Once understanding
    things as small
we better understand
    the large, the all.

…SSG

Little Poems Nine

Sigmund Freud
Employed
Analysis
To treat neurotics who envied phalluses.

poet ee cummings
has financial shortcomings
fails at business enterprises
because he undercapitalizes

Walt Whitman
Was a poet-man
Who claimed we shared an atom
And had been doing so since Adam.

Stephen King, the writer,
Was hit by a careless driver.
King awoke to say, "This is groovy.
I'll make it a book and then a movie."

                                                                    ...LLL

THE FALLEN

Epigraph: "*The feeling is mere bewilderment; I imagine leaves must feel this after they have fallen from a tree until they die.*"
Pvt. T. E. Shaw (aka T.E. Lawrence).

A leaf falls from a tree
Do the other leaves miss it?

Do they remember turning
To share sunlight together,

Do they remember one another's shadows?
The buffet of winds, the fall of rain?

Do they still hear the faint echo?
That was the voice,
As the brittle body breaks beneath a step
The parting as the wind sweeps away?

Do they remember the spring?
When they burst forth
Seeking light, seeking the warmth?

Seasons of living are so brief
And winter comes to all

Do other leaves remember the leaf?
And did they hear it fall?

…JBM

Period

I hate periods
The ends that they imply
the weakness they assert
are certainly a lie

I hate periods
So tiny to the eye
they are barely there
and always they defy

the logic of the mind
Their presence would imply
the thought is over--
a promise I belie

because, it isn't....

I hate periods
I always will

Period

...SSG

FACING REJECTION

WOW!
ANOTHER rejection letter
You must have been devastated.
Time to retire your quill of slurry ink
Slash your wrist, jump off a bridge
Their moat is flooded with Croc-o-gators
Barring your breaching castle walls
The turrets of their lofty fame
Will never unfurl your banner
Ah the disgrace!

So which hurdle or hoop did you ignore?
Did you single or double space?
Did you use the correct font?
Did you rattle and prattle
Three lines too long
I can honestly say
They have never
Rejected
A single line
That I have submitted.
Glowing, cloying, fawning
Well I am too modest to go on
But soon an entire issue to me devoted
Or a back page blurb, when I'm dead and gone.

"Send me your exiles, your tired, your poor,"

Your huddled "gaseous circumlocutions"
(Edwin Newman)

Have you tried the Reader's Digest?
Burnt offal from an unblemished ox?
Now that would get their attention.

Next time you submit something
Try using my name
I've had entire editorial staffs resign
Over that indignity alone

Now they have found another fifty
Of old Joseph Rudyard Kipling's
There goes another season of submissions
To Old White Man's Burden,
Rikki-Tikki-Tavi.

...JBM

prayer takes many forms

knee unbent

standing toe eot with god

words

like tiny fists

pound

against his chest

GOD, DAMN YOU!

melted by love

(fills between space)

goddamnyou

muffled by grace

(fills cracks in faith)

echoes into silence

prayer takes many forms

...LLL

Pliny's Curse

In vino veritas
In wine is truth
Though my observation
Is more often
Deceit and abuse
Squandered fortune
And misspent youth

...JBM

Teeth

In 1968 I took a road trip to see some California hippie friends. When we got settled in, they excitedly told me that I had to meet Dr. Waters.
I said, "Groovy, why?"
They said, "She is the best."
I said, "Groovy. At what?"
They said, "Cleaning teeth."
I said, "Groovy."
The first thing I noticed at her office was the sign that read, "Dr. Sun Rippled Waters, DDS" The second was the stinging sweet smell of incense, which was failing its purpose of masking the odor of pot. Just then Dr. Waters entered. Obviously she was the reason for the incense. She was cloud walking. Yet, her soothing manner and professional skills were excellent. She painlessly and thoroughly cleaned my teeth. She truly was a gentle high dentist.

...LLL

Chapter Ten

When I Go	LLL
Ben Weir	LLL
Mornings	SSG
Weevils	LLL
You Are What You Eat	LLL
Angry Beachgoer	LLL
Choir	LLL
The Burial	SSG
Spring's Tree V	SSG
Little Poems Ten	LLL
Taps	JBM
While Waiting for the Bus & More	SSG
First Day Jitters	JBM
Seems Like Overkill To Me	SSG
A Diabolical Diagram	SSG
Perks	JBM
Humility	JBM
This Is My Poem	SSG

WHEN I GO...

When I go, no one will know I am gone. They will think I have stepped away from my desk on some brief errand. My desk will be one carefully orchestrated red herring. A legal pad, preferably yellow, will be left just so. It will lie at a 45-degree angle to my empty chair. Half a sentence will adorn the first line. Anyone seeing it will conclude I was interrupted in mid-thought – called away by some urgency or another. To reinforce this misconception a newly sharpened #2 pencil will lie at a haphazard angle on the legal pad as if it had just this moment fallen from my hand. Finally, my coffee cup will be missing suggesting that I may have just now stepped away from my cubicle to get a fresh cup. With a proper arrangement of these common props, I can easily be gone for an hour or two while everyone expects me to return momentarily, but when I go, no one will know I am gone.

...LLL

Ben Weir

The Lebanese sky, blue as any in Kansas,
Smelled crisp and sweet like the Gulf coast of Texas.
The morning bustle was well under way
When Ben Weir stepped out to start a new day.
Rough hands grabbed him and snatched him away
Into a waiting car.

Thirty years of missionary service had taught him Arabic.
"On the floor! Get down!" his mind translated. Ben felt sick.
A foot on his neck, exhaust in his nose,
Where they would take him only Heaven knows.
Embassy gates and marine barracks were too easy to forget;
An American civilian was terror's new target--
A minister from the PC(USA)

The Reverend Ben Weir preached peacemaking, not mayhem
He worked for release of hostages before him.
Deploring cruelty and crimes by the state,
He spoke of justice and the Palestinians' fate.
Moved between a number of make-shift jails,
He spent sixteen months in lonely cells.
Constant prayer became Ben's altar.

From what he reckoned to be his Saturday night fare,
Ben wrapped up a corner of bread with care.
He saved it to eat in spiritual communion
With those he yearned to have physical reunion.
Before the sun appeared in the East
He laid out the elements of his communal feast.
He prayed for one more day.

He awaited the light, sometimes a very small light,
Breaking the day from the night.
In the walls where stone met stone shadows appear.
At intersections crosses become clear.
Ben knows that the Light of the World is there
As he kneels in the silence of prayer
At a new day's dawning.

He sees the continuous start of the day
As the sun moves along in its preordained way
From the international dateline
It moves disregarding every borderline –
Indonesia to India,
Europe to Canada
Christians gather to share the Lord's meal.

As dawn breaks on churches visible,
Ben sees the Universal Church invisible.
As into his cell light begins to flood,
He partakes of the body and the blood.
Spiritually united with Christians everywhere,
He finds his burden lighter to bear
Renewing his sense of hope

...LLL

mornings

In the morning
a clear white light
waits outside my window
defining as it goes.

We hope that death
comes the same
a white light
from gentle dawn

clarifying all.

...SSG

Weevils

Two boll weevils were living in a cotton field in North Carolina. One hot summer's day they each decided to strike out on their own and find their fortunes in the world. One found a ride on a semi headed to Philadelphia; the other caught a freight train for New York City. Some years later they met on a busy sidewalk. The first weevil told of becoming the ringmaster for a flea circus. He had traveled the world over and played before royalty. The second weevil confessed that he had been down on his luck for years and had never been successful. Yet, the second insect is the one that is most often remembered. You have, no doubt, heard of the lesser of two weevils.

...LLL

You are what you eat

The emergency room doctor diagnosed an intestinal blockage in an eighty-year-old female patient and ordered x-rays. When the x-rays were read they revealed what appeared to be a fly, inside a spider, inside a bird, inside a cat, inside…

...LLL

Angry Beachgoer

Have you heard about the compulsive man who went to the beach whenever he became frustrated or angry and threw rocks at the birds? He didn't leave a tern unstoned.

...LLL

Choir

A Baptist church from Norman, Oklahoma had a concert choir of some twenty to twenty-five members who, in the course of a year, had collectively lost between five and six hundred pounds by adhering to a diet of low calorie cola and fruit. They were the Norman Tab and Apple Choir.

...LLL

The Burial

They are buried everyday.
Hearts tear, minds shatter,
yet we turn and walk away.

Losers in social roulette's decay
where just a wrist flick matters.
They are buried everyday.

Fast death haunts the highway,
stalks our homes and theaters;
yet we turn and walk away.

Or we shoot before they may
and kill our better natures.
They are buried everyday.

Others come as we delay.
Say good bye to sons and daughters
as we turn and walk away.

God awaits and welcomes daily
those a nation let be slaughtered.
They are buried everyday.

Yet we turn and walk away.

...SSG

Spring's Tree V.

    When I was young in daily games
I hid and sought the shade of trees
    and peeled the bark while seeking fames
I knew someday should come to me.

    I spent a lot of time on roots
while straining breath to touch a branch.
    Or, I'd wait to grow another foot,
to try, this time, a better stance.

    At last, one day, in reaching out
with surer hand of age, I pulled
    the greenest leaves of spring about
my face; so spring could be inhaled.

    I know that breath of spring was sweeter
than any that had come before
    and deem no higher branch much better
for this was spring—I never wanted more.

    ...SSG

Little Poems Ten

Ken Burns,
Preserving histories are his concerns.
He does for the *History Channel*
What teachers once did with boards made of flannel.

Philosopher John Locke
Pedagogues did shock
Posited the infant mind a *tablula rasa*
Until at exam time, it becomes a *tabula erasa*

Thomas Alva Edison
Swallowed hard and took his medicine
900 failures with the electric light
Taught him 900 ways to *not* do it right

Sculptor Gutzon Borglum
Caught in the summer doldrums
Made his stay in Atlanta quite brief
Went to Stone Mountain for a little relief.

...LLL

TAPS

I heard a cricket
Playing "Taps" in the garden
I hope not for us.

…JBM

while waiting for the bus and more

    there is this,
      a tension

between you and in me
a socket full of electricity

      a match
      that waits
        to light

    a rhythm
     an ion
     an icon

  an eon of waiting

until the bus has come

    and gone.

                           ...SSG

FIRST DAY JITTERS AND GALLOWS GOODBYES

We pass through one another's lives so quickly
Line ups, arrest, arraignments
Pre-trial motions
Trials, convictions, sentence hearings
All those whiny victim impact statements
And post-trial appeals

Long lonely bus rides in the night
Another first-day shakedown
Cavity-search shower
Greetings, not like in the old days in person,
Just some pre-recorded tape

That first night on the cell block
First stroll around the yard
What are the other guys like?
What about the guards?

Funny, the things you remember
Your first license plate,
Christmas with no gifts or carols
A Valentine from your cell mate
And all the little bars of soap
Lying on the shower floor

Then it's time for parole hearings
Does anybody ever make their first?
Too soon it's time to say goodbye
To all our new-found friends

Someone always says: You write now!
And we promise we will
Meaning every word
But still we lose touch
We pass through one another's lives so quickly.

...JBM

Seems like overkill to me

Sharp metal jaws
fit exactly to my hand
smooth burgundy plastic
invites my thumb and
fingers to linger
for a moment
to savour the coming kill.

Pity the poor staple
that made the mistake
we so often make
of the wrong place
and the wrong queue.

...SSG

A Diabolical Diagram

the
triangle
is simply the
area of the matrix
times the apex of a
double-cross breeding

...SSG

PERKS

College students
Been sleeping with their confessors
Since Alcibiades was a youth
And Socrates a professor
But of recent
Times have changed
As the teachers moved
To the underaged.

...JBM

HUMILITY

I was a humble child once
An unstudied gracious social art
I learned to tie my shoes
Stand on one leg
Turn somersaults
I got a boo-boo on my knee
And didn't even cry

People told me how clever I was
Agile, athletic and brave
Encouraged I continued
My stellar list of achievements
Learned to read, write
Count, add, subtract
Multiply, divide
And throw a ball

Until I was in the fourth-grade
That's when people got jealous
Petty and mean
When I read, they said
I skipped a word
Said I misspelled
Left out a punctuation mark
Or put too many in
Said I colored outside the lines
Started to choose me
Last for the team

I was a humble child once
It's a gracious social art
That's dying
I ask you
What's the point
Of being humble
If no one pays attention?

...JBM

This is my Poem

This is my poem.
It looks everyday for a home.
Yesterday it sat
under the table
looking up at me.
"Where should I go?"
It asked.
"Where
do you want me to be?"

This is my poem
that seeks to find its place,
a warm spot
by the fire
near your heart.
It curls up
next to my cats
and pretends it has fur.

This is my poem.
It wants you to pet it.
It wants me to place it
where you can see,
where it can be reached.
You see those dark eyes?
It yearns to be
touched by you.

>   ...SSG

Chapter Eleven

ABOUT THE AUTHORS

Jim B. Miller

Jim Miller began creative writing in the tenth year of his schooling in the Midwest. Coming from a large and colorful family he immediately gravitated toward humor and the excesses of that family lore. The collection represented here is the largest published gathering of his works to date. His work history has included all the traditional American fields from grocery sacker to barn painter, from construction to fry cook, and from hotel auditor to Medical Intensive Care in a Trauma #1 Center Hospital. From this background he has drawn upon a range of experience to tell his narrative stories in the meters as broken as the lives they represent with the ever present grace of laughter. If you see yourself or the images of those closest to you in his language and perspective it is to be hoped you join him and his co-authors in smiling at single lines or whole works. He is happy to share the words of encouragement he offers to a paranoid potato and his observations of early morning rituals changed by the recent death of a spouse. Mr. Miller has received numerous prizes throughout his writing career, most from boxes of caramel coated peanuts and popcorn. He has read his monologues and poetry before distinguished audiences; prison inmates both current and former; college professors and their usually failing students as encouragement to change careers and majors. He is currently being sought in several states though this has nothing to do with his poetry.

Sharon S. Gibson

Born in Kansas City, Missouri, Sharon Gibson has not strayed far from home except in her mind. After graduating from the University of Missouri with a major in English she was quick to abandon her graduate work in psychology, later completing her Master's at Webster University. Her first job was at 24 Hi-Way Kiddieland to be followed by ten other trial and error jobs and brief sojourns to Europe. This questionable background led to a twenty-five year career at Truman Medical Center in Kansas City, where she established the first Patient Advocacy program in the metropolitan area. As a result she helped found the Mo/Kan Patient Representative Society serving as both Secretary and President. After retiring from Truman, she started a part time career with H&R Block, managing up to three offices at a time during her ten years with them. No, she does not do taxes; so don't ask. Upon full retirement, Sharon pursued her life long dream of developing her skills as a poet. That dream began at age twelve and continues to this day. She has been published in "Write On", "Seasons To Come" and "Grist". Her poetry was awarded honorable mention in four national/state contests and was recently awarded first place in a Missouri State Poetry Society contest. She is a member of The River Bend Gang chapter of that Society.

Sharon wants to thank Larry Ladd for giving her this opportunity and his wife Karen for tolerating her idiosyncrasies. She is delighted to share space with her friend Jim Miller. The poems in this collection are mostly from Sharon's earlier years--of which there are many. That may explain the tendency toward radicalism and romanticism. Her recent poems have become more morbid and obscure, so if you know someone who likes that sort of thing--and you probably do--tell them to stay tuned for the next collection.

Larry L. Ladd

Born in the boot heel of Missouri during WWII, Larry's earliest memories are of waiting with "Puppa", his non-pedigreed dog, for his father to walk home from work along the mesh wire fence in the front yard. After the war, the Ladd family followed the jobs to St. Louis. They were soon able to join the 1950's exodus to the suburbs. Larry attended the Kirkwood Public Schools and in 1962 enrolled at the University of Missouri in Columbia where he earned his bachelor's and master's degrees from the College of Education. In the late 1960's, he was hired by the Missouri Department of Mental Health as a diagnostic teacher assigned to the Kirksville Regional Diagnostic Center for Mental Retardation. The Jacksonville (Illinois) Public Schools and the Four Rivers Special Education District subsequently hired him as an educational diagnostician and school psychologist. He worked over thirty years in Jacksonville, Illinois where he continues to reside with his wife, Karen. They have two married sons who also live in Illinois, along with two grandchildren and one grand dog. Larry has been active in the Jaycees, Council for Exceptional Children, Habitat for Humanity, Jacksonville Education Association, Christian Marriage Ministry, Special

Olympics, Big Brothers/Big Sisters, and the Boy Scouts of America. He and his wife of 49 years enjoy travel and have visited all fifty states. They are members of the First Presbyterian Church and have participated in and led Bible studies. They have taught classes at Synod School (Synod of Lincoln Trails, Hanover College, Hanover, Indiana) and they lead the Parkinson's Disease Support Group in Jacksonville. Larry was diagnosed with Parkinson's disease in 1994 and admits that he has slowed a bit. He continues to enjoy friends, music (plays the guitar and harmonica—owns a banjo, but it baffles him), dancing (ballroom once or twice a month), woodcarving, fishing, and anything that makes him laugh. He has had one poem published in the Reader's Digest and he finished in third place in a limerick contest sponsored by an Irish pub, but his wife would not let it be included in this book.

C'est fini.

A swordsman and poet named Dennis
Wooed countless young ladies from Ennis.
With a satisfied smile,
One lass said of his style,
"No sword's mightier than his pen is."

...LLL

CPSIA information can be obtained
at www.ICGtesting.com
Printed in the USA
JSHW040327050422
24597JS00001B/21